Study Guide

for

BIAS
AND
THE
PIOUS

Study guide by David B. Kaplan

About the Guide and Its Use: Although this study guide addresses groups, an individual also will find it helpful in (1) identifying the book's primary issues, and (2) providing a way of wrapping up what has been read.

Bias and the Pious deals with a subject appropriate for consideration by groups of adults or teenagers, or by cross-generational groups. *Especially valuable* (although it might take some advance planning) would be a racially mixed group, perhaps involving persons from black and white congregations.

The task of leadership may be shared or rotated, but someone within the group must act as discussion starter and coordinator. Though the leader may change, the leader's aim should be constant,

* to listen to the group's reactions and interpretations of the author's thought, to clarify and/or summarize;

* to make sure the group members take seriously the author's arguments while expressing their own opinions and reactions.

For the group's first meeting a leader should be chosen--one who will have read the entire book and be prepared to introduce it in an enthusiastic way, stimulating interest and curiosity. The leader should also plan for introducing the people to one another so all will feel comfortable in the group.

The guide is intended to be flexible and should be modified by each group according to its interests and needs. For each session there is

1) *an objective* or purpose (the group may wish to revise, re-state, or sharpen the objective).

2) *a series of questions* intended as discussion starters. (If time is a factor, it is wiser to discuss a few in detail rather than try to cover them all.)

3) *a reading assignment for next session* (which may be modified according to time and number of sessions available).

4) *project option(s)*--while not absolutely essential, these are possibilities for making the discussion more vital. The group (or interested individuals) may adopt one of the suggestions or devise its own. These suggestions should be carried out between sessions. When only part of the group is involved, time should be given for a report or summary at the beginning of the following session.

Dittes' study grew out of the concerns researched and reported in *A Study of Generations*.* Those using Dittes' book and this guide will find it most helpful to have that resource available. (Check your local, church, or pastor's library; or order a copy from Augsburg Publishing House.) Chapter 9 and scales 34, 56, and 57 are particularly related to our subject.

Finally, if the sessions are to be more than mere surface airings of opinions, each participant should be willing to make three commitments:

1) to do the assigned reading,

2) to be open and honest with other members in the group,

3) to be supportive of other group members personally although disagreements over specific issues may (and probably will) arise.

---

* *A Study of Generations*. Merton P. Strommen, Milo L. Brekke, Ralph C. Underwager, Arthur L. Johnson. Minneapolis: Augsburg Publishing House, 1972. $12.50.

PREFACE

Don't let the clever-sounding title mislead you: this book deals with a very serious subject. Despite all the teaching about "love your neighbor as yourself," despite the good Samaritan, despite Galatians 3:28, Christians still tend to be--according to Dittes--a rather prejudiced people. Prejudice in the church, moreover, takes some rather subtle and covert forms. Dittes begins by relating four incidents which might conceivably occur in any congregation and which, on the surface, appear to exhibit no particular bias on the part of the people involved. As the author analyzes each incident in some detail, however, it becomes increasingly clear that all are expressions of racist feelings and values.

The source of prejudice among many churchgoers, Dittes contends, is a real need (arising from a defensive life-style) for security from a hostile world. Direct confrontation to counteract prejudice usually only intensifies the person's need and produces polarization. More creative possibilities may be found through dealing with the need itself and supporting the concerned individual. It is to this goal that Dittes directs and challenges us.

I

INTRODUCTION: WHERE WE ARE

Objective: To help us see the extent of prejudicial attitudes in our society, in our congregation, in ourselves.

Discussion:

1. Introductions should be made informally. Each person should tell something about himself--and something about his likes and dislikes.

2. Distribute pencils and paper. The leader should explain that this study deals with prejudice in the church and ask each person to write his own definition of *prejudice*. Discuss these definitions. Is there any consensus? What elements do all (or most) of the definitions have in common?

3. Jot down something about what the Christian church teaches concerning prejudice (recall a biblical passage or story, part of a sermon, a statement by your pastor, or a statement issued by your denomination).

4. Identify some times when actions of Christians have been consistent with the teaching they profess--and situations where they were obviously inconsistent. Cite examples where racial prejudice is reflected in the church. (Why is 11:00 Sunday morning called "the most segregated hour of the week"?)

5. Distribute the study books. Read aloud Dittes' opening comments (pp. 7-8). Subdivide into four buzz groups. Each buzz group should reflect on one of the four incidents described on pages 8-9. To what extent (if any) does the incident express prejudice on the part of the characters involved?

6. Each buzz group should then share with the total group a thumbnail sketch of the incident and the discussed reaction to it.

7. Recall situations in your own life where you have had negative feelings about a person because his race, religion, economic level, or life-style was different from your own. At the time did you sense any conflict between your faith and your feelings? If so, how did you deal with the conflict?

8. What are some reasons why "the pious" may have biased feelings?

Reading Assignment: Remainder of introduction, Chapter 1.

Project Option: Conduct a survey of attitudes in your congregation or community. You might use the questions in *A Study of Generations*, Scales 34, 56, or 57 (pp. 374-375, 386-387); and compare your results with those in the study.

II

WHO ARE THE BIASED?

Objective: To help us understand some of the ways prejudice is expressed in ourselves and others.

Discussion:

1. Before proceeding, it might be helpful to discuss the author's plan of attack. He compares his task to peeling an onion or discovering the hidden mass of an iceberg (p. 10). In terms of the group this may mean bringing to the surface some feelings, values, and attitudes long suppressed. Discuss whether you are willing to risk this possibility--and be open and supportive of each other when it occurs.

2. What was your initial reaction to the incidents--in what ways was it similar to the surface arguments which Dittes advances (pp.13-15)? If you were not willing to dismiss the incidents with those surface arguments, what other factors did you sense were involved?

3. What makes you feel that there was validity in Dittes' second set of arguments (pp. 15-18), showing that the incidents reflected prejudice? What makes it seem that he slanted them to prove his point? How about his contention (p. 18) that, given another set of outward circumstances, the incidents would "almost always come out the same way"? Note the evidence he accumulates to support that contention (pp. 18-22).

4. Cite personal experiences and observations which support the argument that those who are prejudiced against one class, race, or group of people tend in fact to be prejudiced against many differing groups. How may this generalized prejudice or "ethnocentrism" have contributed to the popularity of "All in the Family" or George Wallace?

5. When Dittes suggests that certain mannerisms and expressions are often associated with prejudiced people (pp. 26-27), may he himself be showing prejudice against them? Is it the same as saying, "All Negroes (or Orientals, or Indians) look alike"? If not, what is the difference?

6. Suggest some specific religious values or ideas that a person with a "law orientation" (p. 30) might cherish. Would any of these predispose him toward prejudice? (Do not spend too much time on this question now, since we will be discussing similar questions in detail later.)

7. Picture in your mind a church building (other than the one to which you go). Do you see a structure with solid, massive walls or one with a more open design? Is your mental picture (of the building) related to what you feel the church (as the communion of saints) should be? How would the people involved in the four incidents have been likely to picture a church building (p. 32)?

Reading Assignment: Chapters 2 and 3

Project Options:

A. See *A Time for Burning* (B&W 59 minutes, $20 rental from Augsburg Publishing House), noting especially Dittes' observations about the characters in the film.

B. View "All in the Family." To what extent does Archie Bunker reflect the characteristics described by Dittes in Chapter 1? (Consider viewing this TV program together at someone's home.)

WHY ARE THE PIOUS BIASED?

Objective: To help us understand those needs which give rise to
prejudice, especially among churchgoers.

Discussion:

1. Comment on Dittes' image of a prejudiced person as a "stockade builder" (p. 36). If this image seems appropriate to you,
why? What are some other suitable images? What other factors
might contribute to a person's prejudice?

2. In *Love It or Leave It*?* (pp. 30-32) Jorstad notes that the
pioneer ethic or "manifest destiny" is one of the basic principles of the American creed. To the extent that stockade building
(to keep "us" in and shut "them" out) is part of this ethic,
would you conclude that prejudice is built into our national heritage? Are we in fact promoting it whenever we uncritically rec-
ommend to our young people the values of such an ethic?

3. To some extent all of us are protective or defensive about
our property and relationships. Around what or whom do you find
yourself building stockades? Do you agree with Dittes (p. 42)
that stockade building is actually a form of idolatry? Why, or
why not? Identify some idols.

4. Do you think Luther was stockade building when he wrote "A
mighty fortress is our God"? Notice especially the line in stan-
za 4: "Let goods and kindred go, This mortal life also." If a
person really finds his strength and protection in God, what is
likely to happen to his defensive attitude about other things?

5. How do people in your congregation generally understand the
church: as a structure (external and internal) that must be pre-
served, as a source for identity (see p. 46), or as a servant
community? What evidences are there of a correlation between
their understanding and their biased feelings?

6. What evidence have you found to support the statement that
"there is more racial prejudice in the church than outside of it"
(p. 50)? If you dispute the statement, how do you explain the
evidence which Dittes cites (pp. 50-56)?

7. Dittes claims that "prejudice and churchgoing are both responses to a sense of the precariousness of life" (p. 60). If
churchgoing is thus a response to a felt need, why are many

---

* *Love It or Leave It?--A Dialog on Loyalty*. Erling Jorstad.
Minneapolis: Augsburg Publishing House, 1972. $2.50.

church people "turned off" by the answer the gospel gives? On the other hand, if the gospel demands some openness on the part of a person to receive it, why would prejudiced (and therefore closed) people continue to go to hear it? (These questions will be dealt with in the next chapter, but it's good to explore some possibilities with the group at this point.)

8. Consider the parable of the Pharisee and the tax collector (Luke 18:9-14). What needs did each man have? Who was the stockade builder? What were his idols? Do you see any evidence of prejudice in his prayer? Why do you think he went to the temple?

Reading Assignment: Chapters 4 and 5

Project Options:

A. Read Erling Jorstad's *Love It or Leave It?*, Chapters 2 and 5, for some additional insights into the American religion.

B. Read *A Study of Generations*, Chapter 9, for an evaluation of Lutherans and prejudice.

IV

THE PIOUS DON'T NEED TO BE BIASED

Objective: To help us understand the nature of the Christian faith which frees us from our needs for prejudice.

Discussion:

1. Make sure you understand the difference between prodigal faith and contractual faith, especially in terms of being and doing (pp. 69-70). Some discussion here may be helpful since it is a key issue for Dittes. You may wish to return to the parable of the Pharisee and the tax collector. Who represented a contractual faith? How can you tell?

2. Consider your family relationships--are they governed by a contractual or prodigal style of acceptance? How about business relationships? If both contractual and prodigal relationships have valid applications then, how can we tell where to apply one and where to apply the other? Note the models that Dittes gives (pp. 70-73). We need both grace and works, body and spirit, identity and rules to function as people. Discuss whether the church is primarily a business or a family. How might a clearer understanding of Baptism be helpful?

3. If prejudice is ultimately a theological matter (at least for churchgoers), a misunderstanding of the way God relates to man,

we could expect individuals and denominations who place more emphasis on good works as a means to salvation to show greater prejudice. What evidences are there that this is or is not the case (note Dittes' evidence, pp. 78-80)?

4. Examine once more the prejudice within yourself. Decide whether it is as Dittes suggests (p. 76) related to a contractual inclination, i.e., an addiction to rules and deals.

5. Consider again question 7, Session 3. Might it be that closed individuals want to hear the law preached (as a means to salvation) rather than the gospel (see p. 78)?

6. "Don't bother me with facts, my mind is made up." What does experience tell about the likelihood of being able to argue a person out of strong feelings even when such feelings seem irrational? A role play might be interesting here. Let one person in the group portray one of the characters in Dittes' incidents. Another person should argue with him, openly confronting him with his prejudice. How long does it take for feelings of anger to develop? Show how a congregation could be polarized with such an approach. What are the conditions that would make it worth the risk?

7. How can prejudice reform express a type of contractual understanding? What needs *of the reformer himself* are being met (pp. 90-91)?

8. How does the gospel meet the needs of a prejudiced person? How can it be most appropriately expressed to him (p. 96)? Again a role play would be helpful to involve the group personally in that kind of expression. In terms of the church as a whole or a particular congregation in the midst of a racial crisis, is there time for such an approach?

Project Options:

A. Read Chapters 5 and 6 in *A Study of Generations*.

B. Undertake a supportive ministry to those persons whom your initial survey revealed having prejudiced attitudes.

BIAS
AND THE
PIOUS

BIAS

AND THE

PIOUS

*The Relationship Between
Prejudice and Religion*

James E. Dittes

AUGSBURG PUBLISHING HOUSE
MINNEAPOLIS, MINNESOTA

BIAS AND THE PIOUS

Contents

About This Book

Most people who write about prejudice seem to know for sure what it is. And they also seem sure that it is something their readers have more than they do and something they, as authors, ought to try to scold out of their readers. I am not so sure. I am not even so sure what to label it: bias, racism, bigotry, anti-Semitism, narrow-mindedness, ethnocentrism, intolerance, constricted mind, jaundice, one-sidedness — these are all words that are useful one time or another. Furthermore, I am not so sure where to find prejudice — except to suspect that I can probably find as much in myself as in anyone.

Instead, then, of beginning with a word like "prejudice" and asking "what is it?" and arguing whether or not it is present in this person or that incident, I begin by relating four incidents. This entire book will consist, in a sense, of an exploration of these incidents to discover their significance. We shall peel off layer by layer, to see what different dimensions we can discover in each episode. Or perhaps the metaphor of the iceberg is appropriate here. Some experiences that look ordinary and isolated on the surface may be, in fact, parts of much larger masses that lie below the surface.

Four Incidents

Incident 1. Suppose you are talking to someone about public problems, and he says to you, "Negroes could solve many of their own problems if they would not be so irresponsible and carefree about life." (Three-fifths of the Lutherans in the United States *do* agree with that statement, as *A Study of Generations* tells us.)

Incident 2. Suppose your minister proposes a project in which ten couples from your church, all of them white, would exchange home visits with ten couples, all of them black, from another church. But suppose some people in your church oppose the plan. One objects that December is already too busy for new projects. Another says that the plan is too controversial and will split the church. (Such a proposal was actually made in Augustana Lutheran church in Omaha and received just such objections. This was recorded in the film *A Time for Burning,* produced in 1966 by the Lutheran Film Associates.)

Incident 3. Suppose one Sunday morning a black woman attends your church service, which usually has only white persons present, and later a fellow church member says to you, "I wanted to say hello to her, but didn't quite know how to do it. So I found myself going out the other door." (This is a real experience; it happened in my church.)

Incident 4. Suppose the Christian Education Committee at your church proposes that the one hundred dollars budgeted for "summer conference scholarships" be spent differently this year. Instead of offering ten-dollar scholarships to induce children of your own families to attend, the committee wants to offer a one-hundred-dollar scholarship for an inner-city boy to attend a summer conference. But a member of the trustees objects, "This is money budgeted for Christian education, not for giving away. That's the business of the Benevolences Committee." And another trustee agrees, "I don't think the kids from the city really want to go to these conferences anyway. My daughter said that last summer two colored girls from the Silver Avenue Church were at her conference, and they just stayed off by themselves and didn't want to join in." (This also is based on a real incident.)

How This Book Will Discuss These Incidents

These are the incidents that this book is about. We want to ask several different questions about them and to peel away different layers. We want to ask, first of all, how much significance these incidents have. Are such comments trivial and casual and passing? Or do they have a significance (an effect on the blacks about whom they are spoken and a meaning for the whites who say them) which makes it important for us to consider such incidents, whether we call them "prejudice" or not? What all is happening when people say such things? That is largely the business of the first chapter.

In Chapter 2 we want to peel the onion, or probe deeper in the iceberg, and ask the question of how people come to have these attitudes. Why do people say such things?

Then, in Chapter 3, we face the fact that all of these incidents have occurred in Christian churches. And we also need to face the fact that there is much more evidence of prejudice in churches and among churchgoers. What are we to make of this possibly surprising, possibly disturbing fact?

Chapters 4 and 5 address, in different ways, the question of what to do about it. Where prejudice is found in churches and among church people, what can the church do to overcome it?

I have used the image of iceberg and onion to describe the task of this book, exploring below the surface of certain incidents. But icebergs and onions are unpleasant things; the hidden part of an iceberg can wreck your ship, and peeling an onion can make you cry. The less visible dimensions of these incidents are unpleasant, too. When we say and do the kinds of things described in these episodes, we are injuring other persons in ways that we don't immediately recognize, and we are exposing some very unattractive facts about ourselves. These unpleasant things need to be said as clearly and firmly as possible in the chapters that follow. But having said them, and read them, perhaps we discover that these hidden and unattractive elements are less damaging and less frightening than we supposed — for one important reason: now we can do something about them.

Prejudice: What Is It?

The four incidents represent typical, everyday experiences. Are they casual, harmless, ordinary episodes, with nothing in them worth writing a book about? Do they display dimensions of prejudice that need to be faced? Let us see.

Is Prejudice Present? No.

First, then, the important question about these four incidents: Is there anything present in them that can be counted as *prejudice,* in any important meaning of that term?

There are some important reasons for saying no. First, the people involved would be startled and offended if they were accused of racism or prejudice. "We feel concerned about black people and want them to be treated fairly," they could all honestly say, and they could all undoubtedly point to the outrage they have felt at the poor treatment blacks have received. They would consider themselves liberal on racial issues, not prejudiced. These are just casual passing remarks, the people would all say, not reflecting any underlying negative attitude toward black people. If anything, they would say, their underlying attitudes toward black people are positive. No unflattering opinions were expressed about blacks; they were not called "lazy" or "dishonest," and all the persons present would have resisted such stereotypes if they had been introduced.

The people quoted in these incidents might even say that — far from being prejudiced — their remarks reflect their positive attitudes toward blacks. They really do want blacks to solve their problems (Incident 1); they want a plan of home visits to go well and not be burdened by schedule problems or controversy (Incident 2); they don't want to embarrass a black visitor with an awkward greeting (Incident 3); help for ghetto children through proper channels is better help than impulsive "do-goodism" (Incident 4).

Second, it could be argued that these remarks do not count as prejudice, because no one got hurt. No one was deprived or insulted by anything that was said or done. If black people had been kept out of the church, or out of the summer conference, or really prevented from making or receiving visits, then that might count as prejudice or discriminaton. But, it could be said, no barriers were erected, and the people involved would deny any desire to erect such barriers.

In short, these remarks can't be thought of as racial prejudice, the people might say, because they aren't really remarks about black people at all. They are remarks about the importance of responsibility (Incident 1), about church schedules and procedures (Incident 2), about personal shyness (Incident 3), and about budget policy (Incident 4).

Third, there is none of the distortion or untruth or crude stereotyping that is often the mark of prejudice. People are simply pointing to actual facts: December *is* a busy month; the money *was* traditionally assigned to local church families; the fellow church member *did* feel uncomfortable. The people were not making up things just to express prejudice.

Is Prejudice Present? Yes.

But some other considerations also need to be brought into view. Consider the last point first. The facts cited *are* facts, but they are consistently one-sided, and they are *used* in a one-sided way. If the minister had proposed some other activities, people would not be so suddenly sensitive to how busy December was. The Christian Education committee might have made some proposals that would not have aroused the trustees' concern for the budget so readily. December is not so busy that there isn't always room for one more activity, if people really want to do it. Budgetary traditions bend many times in trustees' meetings, when people want them to. Church members frequently overcome their shyness or discomfort to greet visitors. So these "facts" are solid enough in themselves, but we get the impression that they do not stand by themselves; they are being invoked in the service of something else. That "something else" in these instances — whether it should be called prejudice or not — seems to be avoidance or aversion.

Second, though it may be literally true that no black persons were directly excluded or denied any rights, yet black people *were* affected and so were whites. Each of the episodes has as an outcome the continued separation between the races. Blacks were left out of situations that were under the control of whites. A black child did not attend the summer conference; a black visitor did not return to a white church; visiting was not done between the races; and, the outcome of the attitude in the first incident is that blacks are left to their own devices to solve their problems without the assistance of political and economic forces that are under the control of whites.

To be sure, these situations are not totally under the control of the white people involved; and certainly the outcome is not determined solely by the attitudes and decisions expressed in these incidents. In fact, the people might have said with substantial honesty that they *wanted* to have black persons in their homes and in their congregations and in the summer conference; they might have sincerely said that they felt themselves frustrated by "the way things worked out." Intentions were of the best, so far as there were any intentions.

Yet what the people actually said and did remained consistently on the side of exclusion. Together with many other casual, unintended, and "not prejudiced" remarks and decisions, these episodes contributed to persistent exclusion of black people from situations under the control of whites. In the course of conducting our everyday affairs and making our practical decisions, we almost always end up with the same result: the races remain separate, and blacks are limited in their access to situations and goods which whites control.

It is just such "little" incidents like these that raise the issue of prejudice or exclusion. We can say that we are ready to take a strong stand for racial justice and equality, whenever that issue may confront us. But such clear confrontations seldom come our way. The issues of justice and equality come embedded in everyday practical affairs. We must attend to these practical issues, sometimes without even seeing the questions of racial fairness or respect involved, and seldom seeing these questions clearly enough to deal with them. But we continue to have an impact on racial issues as we go about making practical decisions in which the relations of whites and blacks are involved only incidentally — yet decisively.

It is just this persistent racial exclusion in everyday affairs, despite conscious personal attitudes to the contrary, that leads some writers to say that racial preju-

17

dice is built into the "structure" of society. That may be one helpful way of thinking about the matter. But I find it more helpful to think about it as I have put it above: whenever we consciously and deliberately confront a question that we regard as an issue of racism, we are likely to decide it in favor of equality and fairness. But at the same time, everyday decisions which we don't think of as involving racial fairness can nevertheless accumulate to have a substantial impact against openness and justice between races.

"Isolated" Incidents Accumulate

For there *is* an accumulative effect of our remarks and decisions, and it is one-sided. These four incidents are isolated ones which "just happen" to come out on the side of further exclusion, we might like to say. "Another time it might come out differently; questions of budget and calendar might work out to favor openness and not exclusion," we also might like to say. But it almost always comes out the same way. The same people whose remarks and decisions happen to "look" prejudiced in these episodes are likely to show attitudes and behavior on other occasions which also happen to "look" prejudiced. Even when our intentions are really good and not prejudiced, we still come up with actions and attitudes that look as if they *were* guided by prejudice.

In the Omaha church (*A Time for Burning*) there was another incident, separate from the proposal for exchange of home visits. Teenagers exchanged visits to each other's classes and worship services. People who were opposed to the home visits on various "non-prejudiced" grounds (December is a busy month; it would upset the church) now found themselves objecting to the visit by black teenagers to their church. This time the grounds were also "not prejudiced," and they were in themselves legitimate (they objected to the procedures; there should have been more warning or consultation in advance). But the effects still accumulated as though they *were* governed by prejudice.

The same woman who was made uncomfortable by the black visitor once attended a Sunday evening combined service with a black church. She apparently found the style of worship odd in ways that she could not respect. She made a point of writing "sermon" in quotation marks when she described the service in a note to a friend and referred to the "so-called worship" on another occasion. She was not able to accept a style of religious expression meaningful and natural to the blacks. Her objections to the service might have been made on grounds entirely separate from race, just as the discomfort she felt about welcoming the visitor might have seemed based on grounds other than her race. But after a while, the accumulated effect of such incidents is the same as if they had all been governed by racial bias.

In the same church at which the trustees opposed the summer camp proposal — let us call it the Bethany Church — there were other incidents that year involving some of the same people. There was an exchange of choirs arranged just when many members of the white choir — for different and genuine reasons — found it inconvenient to attend rehearsals. "I was going to have to drop out for awhile anyway," they said and meant it. "This just seemed to be the only time we could arrange the exchange," said the director. "We needed our full choir for our own services during Advent, and again to get ready for Lent." Indeed, that does seem a reasonable and practical decision, untainted with any recognizable prejudice — though it does have overtones of sharing "second-best" with the other church.

Then there was the time when many persons in the Bethany church neighborhood used the church library for several planning meetings; most were members of the church and some were trustees. What they were planning was opposition to a proposal to open in the neighborhood a half-way house for delinquent boys. "We have nothing against these boys because they are colored," several men felt the need to repeat, and undoubtedly they meant it. They didn't feel any racial prejudice and wouldn't have tolerated anyone saying that blacks should be excluded from the Bethany neighborhood. But the facts were that most of the intended residents were white. The men had erroneously supposed that "delinquent boys" meant "black boys." Somehow, after the intended racial balance became known, fewer men found it convenient to come to the evening protest meetings; and those who did come didn't make such fear-filled speeches about the "dangers these delinquents pose to our own children, especially our girls." The half-way house was eventually opened. "Promising to keep down the ratio of blacks was the only way we could get our house open," explained the sponsors, proud of their strategy.

So experiences do accumulate with mounting and one-sided consequences for both races. Attitudes which are "prejudice-like" if not actual "prejudice" get entrenched and expressed, and exclusiveness persists — all despite the fact that racial attitudes and issues of exclusiveness are never directly addressed. People cite different reasons and different motives from one situation to another, but it often seems that bits of ice on the surface are indeed moving together and that what must keep them together is some persistent avoidance of members of another race. Does this deserve to be called "prejudice"?

This consistency can be seen in reports from researchers, as well as in the kinds of anecdotes we have been recounting. Consider the remark quoted as Incident 1: "Negroes could solve many of their own problems if they would not be so irresponsible and carefree about life." People who express that attitude may be concerned primarily with public problems and with questions about responsibility. It is possible that this remark does not indicate any biased, or fearful attitude toward black people. But in the survey entitled, A Study of Generations, people who agreed with that remark are also likely to object to blacks and whites dating each other and to favor segregation of blacks from whites. Social scientists consistently find that a person who acts in an exclusive way in one situation involving a black person also acts that way in other situations; and a person holding an unfavorable attitude toward one particular black person is far more likely to feel in a similar way toward other black persons in other situations. There is something guiding his thinking and behavior across many different kinds of situations, and that "something" looks like prejudice, even if it is not "really" prejudice.

Is Archie Bunker Real?

But now let us peel another layer away. Let us see if the iceberg is even larger. Are there other spots of ice moving in the same threatening way and perhaps all connected under the surface? If someone makes remarks like those quoted in our four incidents, we have said that he is more likely than not to express similar exclusive and negative judgments about black people in other situations. But what about groups other than racially different groups?

The portrayal of Archie Bunker in TV's *All in the Family* is based on a highly generalized prejudice — negative opinions and excluding judgements about all people who are recognizably different. Is this portrayal truth or fiction? Research shows that it is far more truth than fiction. A person expressing negative attitudes toward blacks is far more likely than not to express similar negative attitudes toward many groups with different ethnic backgrounds and different life styles.

In America, for example, the Ku Klux Klan represents an entrenched attitude that has been equally anti-Jew, anti-Catholic, and anti-black. *A Study of Generations* found that negative attitudes towards blacks were correlated with negative attitudes towards Jews. Persons who express "prejudice-like" attitudes towards blacks are more likely to say things like "Jews don't care what happens to anyone but their own kind," or "Jews have a lot of irritating faults." The authors concluded that they had measured what they called a "generalized prejudice," a conclusion also reached by other researchers.

Research studies which have started with anti-Semitism rather than with racial prejudice have come to the same conclusion. Wherever they start on the surface, they find the same iceberg. Perhaps the most famous study of anti-Semitism, *The Authoritarian Personality,* found that antagonism towards Jews was closely correlated with antagonism towards Negroes or "Japs," or "Okies," or foreigners in general, or "Zoot-suiters," or "certain religious sects who refuse to salute the flag." To express this same idea of a general prejudice, the authors adopted the word "ethnocentrism."

One recent research study, *Christian Beliefs and Anti-Semitism* by Charles Glock and Rodney Stark, yielded some evidence of the correlation between anti-Semitism and racial prejudice. However, since the authors were attempting to support a theory that applied only to anti-Semitism and not to racial bias, it is understandable why they tended to deemphasize the correlation. They do not report in their book the correlation between their measure of anti-Semitism and their measure of racial prejudice. But Table 62 in their book shows significant relation between their measure of "religious bigotry" (which is chiefly composed of anti-Semitic items) and such racially bigoted statements as "It's a shame Negroes are so immoral."

Some researchers (for example E. L. Hartley in *Problems in Prejudice*) have even asked people about attitudes towards non-existing groups such as "Daniereans," or "Pireneans," or "Wallonians." Obviously, a negative attitude toward such a non-existent group must be attributable to the underlying iceberg of prejudice, since it has no basis in actual experience. High correlation has been found between negative attitudes toward such non-existent groups and toward Jews or Communists or "labor union members."

Archie Bunker expresses attitudes not only about other kinds of persons, but also about current social issues. But it is hard to make this distinction very neatly, because he often expresses his attitudes about *issues* in terms of attitudes toward *groups* such as "anti-war bums," or "welfare chiselers." In any case, the iceberg does seem to extend.

Social scientists have been systematically asking about attitudes on public issues since the 1930s when — interestingly enough — some of the most common topics concerned war, divorce, capital punishment, abortion, socialized medicine, rehabilitation of prisoners, and welfare. In general, it is likely that somebody will prove "conservative" or "liberal" on most of these issues if he is "conservative" or "liberal" on one of them. This is what researchers find.

It is also true that more conservative attitudes on these issues are correlated with more restricted and prejudice-like attitudes on racial issues. To be sure, the correlation is not perfect. There are many non-prejudiced individuals with conservative social views, and vice versa. But the correlation is more likely than not. The study of anti-Semitism referred to earlier, *The Authoritarian Personality,* found that attitudes on political and economic issues were predicted by attitudes on anti-Semitism or "ethnocentrism." *A Study of Generations* found that there was a correlation between "generalized prejudice" and the "social distance" that people wanted to put between themselves and a variety of groups representing attitudes on many different issues. These included Communism, homosexuality, drugs, radical politics, alcoholism, mental illness, and divorce.

Styles of Mind

Now let us peel off an especially important layer. So far we have talked about *what* attitudes people have, what opinions they hold towards other persons. Now we turn to the question of *how* they hold these attitudes. We often speak of a prejudiced person as a "closed-minded" or "narrow-minded" person. Is there a particular style of mind or style of life that seems to go along with prejudice-like and conservative attitudes?

What if you watched the film *A Time for Burning* but left the sound track off? Can you tell from the *way* people behaved and from the *way* they expressed themselves *what* they are saying on the question of the proposed racial visits? I think that you can, or at least I think that I can. Some of the people in the film show more stiffness of posture than others, more tightness of face, especially around the mouth. They have a more chopped or clipped way of speaking. They hold their arms stiffly at their sides or use their hands in chopped, abrupt gestures. If we could listen to the tone of what they were saying, without understanding the words, we would sense a firmness and finality — some might even say dogmatism or authoritarianism — in the way they were speaking. This stiffness is more apparent because it contrasts with the manner of other persons in the film who tend to be more slouched in posture, perhaps leaning forward with their head in their hands, perhaps with their hands in their pockets, or moving their hands in more flowing gestures; they tend to speak in lower pitched less tense voices, in more flowing, less stiff fashion.

If we watched the film with the sound off and supposed that most persons behaving stiffly were against visits and conversations among persons of different races, we would be right most of the time. (This would include also the black barber who displays the same stiffness of person and of speech and who also opposes conversations and visits between races.) We would not be right in every instance; there are exceptions. But there *is* a tendency for rigidity of person to be associated with conservatism of attitudes. Prejudiced persons tend to hold tight to their outlook and to build fences around themselves, building fences not only with what they believe but in the way they express it.

The woman who had trouble in greeting the church visitor is known for her concern for propriety. She is very carefully dressed and always addresses others quite formally. She has been known to object when liturgical hangings were inadvertently left the wrong color and to object to other liturgical improprieties. One of the Bethany trustees who was most concerned with the budgetary adjustment proposed by the Christian Education committee is someone who is scrupulously concerned with the church's budget at every point. He queries the church treasurer regularly and insists on exactness. These patterns do not really surprise us. We expect people who are concerned with exactness and who conduct themselves with scrupulous propriety, sometimes even stiffness, to have difficulty crossing racial and other boundaries.

Two researchers, Russell Allen and Bernard Spilka, made a careful effort to discover which persons seem to be relatively open and which persons are relatively closed in the way their minds work. They conducted tape-recorded interviews on the subject of religion, and then asked fellow researchers to listen to the tapes and to judge *how* each person expressed himself. Separately, they also obtained measures of the degree of prejudice expressed by each person. They discovered that those who were more prejudiced did demonstrate a distinctive style in the way their minds seemed to work when they were discussing religion. On the opposite page are some of the phrases the researchers used to describe the most important differences they found.

It is significant that the authors of the famous study on anti-Semitism began by examining attitudes towards Jews, but ended up calling their report *The Authoritarian Personality*. They found that anti-Semitism was not only correlated with general prejudice towards various minority groups, but also correlated with other styles and habits of mind. Much of this style is characterized by their labels of rigidity, intolerance of ambiguity, undue "concreteness," and "stimulus-boundness." They found that the more prejudiced persons could not shift easily from one kind of problem or one set of ideas to another.

In my own research, I have assessed such styles of mind by asking people to listen to a tape recording with not very distinct sounds, or to read a prose passage with some phrases garbled. I have found that some persons — those "intolerant of ambiguity" — were more likely to assert what the indistinct sounds or garbled phrases meant. And they were never right.

MORE PREJUDICED	LESS PREJUDICED
Detached-Neutralized: Religion is considered thoroughly important, but is mainly severed from substantial individual experience or emotional commitment. Ideals remain abstracted from specific behavior and rarely realistically influence daily activities.	*Relevant:* Religiosity is a matter of personal concern and central attention. There is an emotional commitment to religious ideas, ideals, and values. Ideals and values incorporated in the religious beliefs seem to account for or be relevant to daily activities.
Restrictive: Relatively inaccessible or closed to differing ideas. Tends to restrict admissability of different beliefs or practices. Apparently tries to narrow or encapsulate religiosity by rejection, distortion, or a "screening out" of different ideas and practices.	*Candid-Open:* A relatively greater tolerance for diversity. A frank, straightforward approach to the evaluation of similar or different ideas and practices.
Concrete-Literal: Religiosity seems to be rooted in concrete, tangible, specific, or literal statements and judgments. Practical, observable referents and concrete, graspable images used in preference to more philosophical ideas.	*Abstract-Relational:* Religiosity seems to be largely anchored in abstract principles, intangible ideas, and relational expressions. There is use of general categories, philosophical notions, or formulated theology.
Monopolistic - Dichotomous: Religiosity is composed of a relatively small number of categories or elements.... Language seems to be based on bipolar ideas and "two-valued" judgments.	*Differentiated:* Religiosity tends to be composed of a relatively large number of categories or elements.... Ideas tend to be multiple rather than simple, global, or overgeneralized.

29

Others were more able simply to report that they couldn't understand the sounds or the passages.

Also as part of "the authoritarian personality" are such characteristics as these: When things go wrong, the authoritarian (that is, the prejudiced) person is more likely to blame other persons than himself, or he is more likely to try to forget the problem and keep busy than he is to try to think about it and solve it. He is more likely to be concerned about his own status and success. He is more likely to think of himself in relatively "glorified" terms. That is, he tends to describe himself as virtuous and able and talented and full of accomplishment, rather than in more balanced and realistic terms. Apparently, people who are closed-minded in the way they think about others are also closed-minded in the way they think about themselves.

A Study of Generations found that prejudice was highly correlated with two characteristics which defined what the study called law orientation. One of these was called "need for unchanging structure" and was represented by agreement with such items as, "If I were to follow my deepest concern, I would concentrate on trying to preserve the very best of a long tradition. This seems to me to be a primary need today." Or, "When you are young, you can afford to be an enthusiastic supporter of reform and change, but as you grow older, you learn that it is wiser to be cautious about making changes." The other characteristic was called the need for religious absolutism. It is represented by agreement with such items as, "The

30

true Christian is sure that his beliefs are correct," or "I like to think that Christians all over the world are going through nearly the same liturgical service in their public worship."

Gordon Allport in *The Nature of Prejudice* describes the style of mind of prejudiced people. "Prejudiced people seem afraid to say 'I don't know.' To do so would cast them adrift from their cognitive anchor. . . . Prejudiced people demand clear-cut structure in their world, even if it is a narrow and inadequate structure. Where there is no order they impose it. When new solutions are called for they cling to tried and tested habits. Wherever possible they latch onto what is familiar, safe, simple, definite."

Styles of Personal Relations

But let us peel off still one more layer. In our consideration of style of mind and style of thinking we found a closed-mindedness correlated with prejudice. This is not to say, of course, that there is not some closed-mindedness among some people who propose liberal racial attitudes; there is also a "dogmatism of the left" as well as a dogmatism of the right. But here we are concerned to look at those characteristics that seem to go with prejudice.

What about style of relations with other persons? We find that there is not only a constriction of mind connected with prejudice, but there is also a constriction of relationships. This is not too surprising, since one of the meanings of prejudice is that people are setting boundaries around themselves and between themselves and others. But we find this to be true not only between the prejudiced person and those of other ethnic groups, but also between a prejudiced person and *most* other people.

In *A Study of Generations,* one of the items that most defines the "need for unchanging structure" (which is correlated with prejudice) is this: "The best way to improve world conditions is for each man to take care of his own corner of the vineyard." For some of the people in our four incidents this is mostly what belonging to the church seems to mean: the church is a place where they can more or less huddle together, setting clear boundaries between themselves and those outside the church. As we have already pointed out, part of being an "authoritarian personality," is to have highly idealized views of oneself, one's parents, and others very close around him. Another move by the "authoritarian personality" is to draw sharp boundaries between this "in" and "good" group and those who are outside and blameable for most of the ills of the world. Another part of being an "authoritarian personality" is to have a very high regard for structure and hierarchy in society.

So, when we see a trustee agitated about giving church money to an outside boy, or when we see a woman distressed about greeting a black visitor, we are seeing not just a narrowly directed prejudice against a particular kind of "outsider." We are also seeing evidence that such persons have built elaborate stockades all around their lives, and any intrusion or breaching of those stockades will be upsetting.

Prejudice represents the wall between oneself and a particular group of persons. That one wall is really part of an entire stockade some of us find it necessary to build, not only against one group but against all groups, a protective wall encircling our lives, section by section, until we are totally and safely closed in as much as possible, and the threats of life are closed out.

But to begin to use words like *protect* and *threat* and *safe* is to anticipate what we must discuss next: *why* do we go about building these stockades?

2

Prejudice: Why Is It?

A prejudiced attitude tells us much more about the person who holds it than about the one at whom it is directed.

If I tell you that Negroes are lazy, or violent, or irresponsible, or destructive of property and of property values, or always better off in their own churches and camps and neighborhoods, then you might reply by telling me that my opinions simply don't match the facts about black people. And you would be right. One of the reasons that we use the word "prejudice" for such negative stereotypes is exactly that: the opinions do *not* come from the facts but from some prejudgment.

Furthermore, you would be right if you went on to say that such attitudes are not only inaccurate, but are also *unfair* to black people. Such prejudice is wrong. It is wrong factually and it is wrong morally. Black people are deprived of a fair place in society, and I am deprived of some important human relationships when I hold such prejudiced opinions and express them by creating or maintaining social barriers.

Safely Enclosed

But you would also be right to go on and say that even though my remarks do not provide an accurate picture of black people, they do begin to provide a picture of *me*. You can know that I am a *stockade-builder*. Such negative opinions are a way of separating myself from black people and of excluding them from my society — at least in my mind and in my talk. Such opinions are planks in a stockade. But if I undertake such separation and exclusion in my mind and in my talk, I probably also do in fact. So far as I can, I tend to exclude black people from my neighborhood or church or school.

Beyond this, you can know that I not only exclude blacks, but that I am also very likely to exclude almost any other recognizably different group — different ethnically, or different in life style, or different in values and outlook on life. And not only different groups of people, but different ideas — unflattering or probing questions about myself, changes in ways of thinking and doing things, even desirable changes, insignificant errors, or necessary ambiguities. Until, finally, I have a complete stockade built around my life. I am fully enclosed. I am safely enclosed.

If you see just one plank ("Negroes should be more responsible," or "I couldn't quite bear to greet the colored visitor," or "December is too busy for interracial visits," or "We should spend the church's money for the church's purposes") then you might suspect that the builder of one plank is also the builder of an entire stockade.

Why has this stockade been built? That is the subject of this chapter. In the first chapter we recognize how fully enclosed the prejudiced person is. This chapter is to help us realize how important it is to him that he is *safely* enclosed.

If I am prejudiced, or in other ways have enclosed and constricted my life, it is because I *need* my prejudice. We can deplore the fact that I need the prejudice — just as we properly deplore the bad effects of the prejudice itself. And in the last chapter we will try to discover ways to make prejudiced persons not need their prejudice. But for the moment, unless we are to close ourselves off from some important facts about prejudiced persons, we need to recognize that need for prejudice.

Why do people build stockades? Because they have something inside which they feel is ultimately precious and because they fear dangerous threats from the outside. What they have is precious and precarious.

Fear of Lurking Threats

"My first reaction when I think of the future is to be aware of its dangers." This is one of the items in

A Study of Generations most closely related to the measures of prejudice. Another item closely associated with prejudice, this one showing the same mentality applied to protecting a church, was "We Christians have to exercise caution when we act in the local community, because it is so easy for those outside the church to misinterpret what we are trying to do." Prejudiced persons apparently think of themselves as early settlers on this continent did, as aliens perpetually threatened with being engulfed by a hostile world. They must hurriedly build a strong stockade, for enemies lie just beyond it. (If this is also the way to describe the mental outlook of a person who finds himself unable to live with the trust and faith of one who feels himself in a world ruled by a sovereign and merciful God, then we have a clue to pick up later in the book as to how religious faith might undo prejudice.)

This mentality is shown explicitly in a study by Allport and Kramer, "Some Roots of Prejudice." They found that prejudiced persons were more likely to agree with this statement, "The world is a hazardous place in which men are basically evil and dangerous." *A Study of Generations* also found prejudice related to a pessimistic outlook on life.

In the Augustana church *(A Time for Burning)*, those opposing the racial visits are quick to point to the threat of "upheaval" and "upset" and "breaking the church wide open." They are ready to see disaster far beyond the proportions of the immediate question at hand.

One of the trustees of the Bethany Church who opposed the $100 camp proposal has equipped his house with an expensive burglar alarm and has bought a gun. Some of us in this modern day build stockades around our homesteads quite as literally as did our frontier ancestors. Apparently we still feel like alien intruders in an unfriendly and unwelcome land.

It is worth noticing the times and places at which racial prejudice and discrimination become strongest. The principal clue as to who becomes prejudiced toward whom, and when, is found in patterns of social and economic competition and precariousness. Prejudice is most rampant in the South among white people who have minimal income and minimal property and who face constantly the threat of economic disaster. And prejudice is strongest in northern cities among those who have most recently left the ghetto themselves and who are now established with a house in the suburbs, heavily mortgaged and furnished on credit, those with the most slippery toehold on the American ladder of success. Those who feel they are still at the frontier need most of all to find ways to establish and entrench their precarious position, and these ways include prejudice and discrimination against those who are closest behind.

In times of greatest economic threat and scarcity we see the most stockade building. It is no accident that the early years of the 1970s brought both economic downturn and unemployment and also a retrenchment in various gains of civil rights that black people had won in the '60s. This retrenchment is also related to the gains themselves. As a minority group makes gains in employment and education, it became all the more threatening to groups just ahead of it, especially in bad times. Northerners are quite liberal on issues of civil rights, so long as those issues remain in the South, but find it a different matter when civil rights come north.

Protecting Our Precious Possessions

When white men first landed on this continent, they were truly "on their own." Their feeble resources of tools, food, supplies, and manpower meant the difference between life and death. Without these supplies and each other, they were nothing and needed to be protected at all costs. So they built a heavy stockade, like the one which can be seen in replica at Jamestown.

The tribes of Israel, the Old Testament tells us, did it differently. They found themselves able to put their ultimate trust in their Lord God, represented for them in their wanderings by the Ark of the Covenant. *This* is what they protected as fiercely as they could. Since they were on the move, they could hardly build a stockade, but they constructed the psychological equivalent in the form of a taboo: the Ark simply must not be touched! In all times and places, what men and women most rely on and most value they regard as holy; and what they regard as holy, they most vigorously protect. "Where your treasure is, there will your heart be" — and also whatever stockade or taboo or other protection you can construct. What do people count on these days, and treat as holy, and therefore need to protect — perhaps with the devices of prejudice?

Property. Property, especially "private property," as we have learned to say with a kind of awe, has always played a special role in the American dream. Americans have used property as a way of measuring a person's value. The phrase "personal worth" has come to mean a person's financial worth, and especially his private property. The first white settlers in this land were prompted, in large measure, by their desire to establish domain over their own land. As the frontier was pushed back, it became important to each man to establish his own land claim. The promises and the status of becoming a landowner or a homeowner continue to lure people, beyond financial gain or even beyond financial wisdom, into the suburbs, into mortgages, and into mail-order purchases in Vermont or Florida or Arizona.

Landowning or homeowning is one of the last privileges we now accord rising minority groups. Even where suitable housing is provided for minority persons, we arrange it so that they still are tenants, rather than permitting them to purchase their apartments and enter the class of homeowners. We arrange things this way, even though we frequently argue that such tenants do not show responsibility for the property, because they are only tenants. If we really meant that, we should encourage them to purchase.

"Property value" is one of the things most frequently and fiercely protected from intrusion by minority groups. One Omaha church leader in *A Time for Burning* explicitly raised the question of "property values." He conjured up the threat of interracial visits leading to integrated neighborhoods, where the blacks would fail to maintain their property and eventually depress neighborhood property values. Despite evidence of real-estate studies that integration does not depress property values, this fear continues among many people. It is perhaps related more to the loss of prestige in homeowning than to fear of actual financial loss. The status *is* lost if it has to be shared with "others."

In summary, property becomes for many of us an idol or false god. As a *god* it seems to promise salvation — assurance of worth and a place in the universe. But because it is a *false* god, only an idol, it needs to be protected and saved more than it can save. And one of the ways we protect this idol, along with scrupulous lawn tending and zoning vigilance, is with resistance to strangers in our neighborhood — or in our church or schools or place of work. This idol is too precious, but also too precarious, for us to take a chance. So we fall more deeply into the trap that all idol worship sets for us: once we begin to rely on the idol, we need what it can do for us; but once we come to trust and need it, we must be all the more careful to protect it. So we become addicted, idolatrously, to various means of protection, including our prejudices.

Children. The other precious and precarious idol common to many of us is our children. We have a heavy investment in our children, emotional not just financial, and we count on them to become something and to do something. Their accomplishments and achievements will offer a vicarious "salvation" for us. We count on our children to make good for us. But if our property proves unable to deliver the satisfactions it seems to promise, our reliance on our children is even more precariously placed. They have their own lives to live; their primary business is not to provide "salvation" for their parents.

So most of us are caught with needing to find ways, as far as we can, of protecting our children's path. Our protection often assumes the proportions of a mammoth stockade, shielding them from all dangers — real and imagined.

It is hardly any accident, then, that the episodes that trigger our racial vigilance frequently involve our children. The integration of schools is threatening because it is easy for us to exaggerate the dangers to our children. We are quick to anticipate "inferior education" dragged down by the "lower-class average," or to foresee "lives wrecked by interracial marriages for which society is not ready."

In the Augustana Church of Omaha it was the visiting of black young people that precipitated an emotional crisis for many. Some drove away from church that morning as soon as they saw the black youth. My guess is that the visit of black young people was more upsetting than a visit of black adults. Similarly, in the Bethany Church, the proposal for spending $100 was a step toward integration of young people. Here my guess is that the proposal for spending that amount on a black adult project would not have aroused as much concern for budgetary propriety.

Our children arouse escalated protective instincts, especially when we are counting on them to make good for us, and especially when we begin to recognize that it may not happen that way. Our own fear of racial integration among our children may be a measure of how much we have come to treat them as gods promising us "salvation," or a measure of how much we have come to recognize that they are, for us, false gods.

Image. Along with property and children, "image" is an important word in American culture — and "self-image." It matters a great deal how others see us and how we see ourselves. The woman who found herself leaving by a back door, rather than greeting a black visitor in church, prides herself on her social grace. Apparently she felt that her mastery over this social situation was threatened by the prospect of having to greet a person with different patterns of behavior and expression. And rather than risk her trusted but precarious self-image, she left by another door.

44

When I watch the film *A Time for Burning* I get the impression that some of the church officials were engaged in a subtle power battle with the minister, and perhaps he with them. There seems to have been a contest as to who was in charge of the church and its program. The minister seems intent on teaching his lay leaders on the basis of his special training and experience. And the lay leaders seem equally intent on teaching the minister, out of their accumulated experience and wisdom, how things are properly done. They particularly insist on doing things in good order, which means slowly. People do derive a sense of self-assurance from the "image" of being wise and experienced. Perhaps such a self-image is already part of the stockade. In any case, it too needs to be protected from threatening novelties and intrusions.

Many such people seem to function with grace and confidence as long as they keep their world small enough. The woman who did not greet the visitor was at her best in small women's groups in the church. Men can often manage and master matters in the relatively small and familiar confines of church business. Any prospect of widening these groups threatens the confidence and competence they have established.

The Church and Other Idols. The church itself frequently becomes a kind of idol. Perhaps because it provides the small supporting group just described, perhaps for other reasons, people come to invest themselves heavily in the church organization and to rely on it for rewards. In *A Time for Burning* people repeat over and over again the importance they attach to preserving the church organization and membership as it is. We do not get many particular clues as to just *what* importance the church has for some of these persons. But we do know that some people get a major share of their identity from participation in the church organization. "Who are you?" we may ask someone and get the answer, "I am the chairman of the congregation." When people rely on the church organization and their offices in it for a major portion of their identity, it is no surprise that they find it necessary to protect this organization and these offices from disruption.

Then there are the idols of business success and of marital happiness and all of the others by which we live and from which we hope to receive blessed assurance. It is because we do rely on all of these idols, and because they are so unreliable, that we are constantly finding ourselves hard pressed and needing to build new stockades. This is why so many of us so much of the time fit so easily the picture given in the first chapter. We make our many defensive maneuvers and spend far more of our energies building protective fences around ourselves than we do opening ourselves up.

In trying to understand why and how we become prejudiced, I have emphasized our *need* for the prejudice. It does something for us that we apparently need to have done. I have said this to try to understand the prejudice, but not to excuse it or condone it. In fact, the primary reason for exploring our needs for prejudice is so we can do a better job of getting rid of our prejudice. When we attack the prejudice, in ourselves or in others, and try to scold or threaten it away, we seldom succeed. It is because our scolding and our threatening only enhances the need for the prejudice. It seems to me that if we are going to undo the prejudice, we must *undo* the need for the prejudice, not enhance the need. It is to this end that the last two chapters of this book will build directly on this chapter.

But first we need to peel still one more layer and discover another set of characteristics that seem to go with prejudice. Of all things, this is churchgoing, and the next chapter will propose that churchgoing is something else we may do because we "need" to and that is as it should be. Because our "need" for prejudice and our "need" for churchgoing is frequently the same, it will be no surprise that churchgoing seems to go along with prejudice.

3

Especially in the Churches

So far everything that has been said about prejudice could be said about prejudice wherever it is found in our society. Yet the illustrations used throughout the discussion are all of persons who are in churches, and the aim of this book is to give special attention to the relationship between religion and prejudice. In this chapter we focus on prejudice as it is found among those of us who are churchgoers.

Why write especially about this? Why give special attention to churchgoers who are racially prejudiced than to members of any other group — steel workers, Chamber of Commerce merchants, non-churchgoers— who are racially prejudiced?

One reason is that it seems especially disconcerting to find racial prejudice in the Christian church. Christian faith is the contradiction of everything prejudice stands for. Christian faith proclaims the oneness of mankind; prejudice separates men. Christian faith seeks to make life fuller and richer; prejudice narrows and constricts men's lives, both those who are the objects of prejudice and those who are prejudiced. Christian faith proclaims the sovereignty of God over all men's lives; prejudice sets some men up to be sovereign over others. Christian faith casts out fear; and prejudice breeds on fear. Christian faith proclaims the foolishness of putting our trust in worldly idols of our own making; prejudice is a way of protecting and worshiping those idols. So it is especially disturbing to find evidence of racial prejudice among those of us who profess the Christian faith. We, more than others, should be concerned and able to rid ourselves of this affliction. This, then, is one reason for wanting to give special attention to racial prejudice among churchgoers.

But there is another and more disturbing reason. Not only is racial prejudice especially incongruous in the church; the uncomfortable but well-established fact is that *there is more racial prejudice in the church than outside of it.* Racial prejudice — and all of the states of mind going with racial prejudice — is more likely to be found among churchgoers than among people who are not churchgoers. That has been the consistent finding of researchers who have studied this question over many years in this country and others. As we continue to analyze prejudice, one of the things that we find, more likely than not, is membership in a Christian church.

Because I am a churchgoer, my first reaction on hearing this information was to challenge it. "It can't be so," I thought. "Someone is trying to attack the church this way. Look at all the fine, unprejudiced, gentle persons I know in church, and look at all the good work against prejudice done by church people, especially statements by national leaders and official agencies of the churches." That is what I wanted to think, and as far as it goes, that is true.

But other facts are too overwhelming to be denied. Look at what happened to Reverend Youngdahl in the Augustana Church (A Time for Burning). When he proposed a very modest program of interracial visits in the homes, and when he condoned one visit by black teenagers from a nearby church, he was compelled to resign. The pressure came from people within the church. Church leaders more often arouse the hostility than the support of church people when they take strong stands for integration or for support of blacks. Mission and service activities of Protestant denominations in the U.S. are suffering financially, partly because church people have withheld contributions from national denominational agencies in retaliation for the support denominational leaders have given to black movements.

As a miniature example of this problem, consider whether the Christian Education committee of the Bethany Church is likely to have easy going the next time it presents its annual budget proposal to the trustees. Consider the difficulty one white church member had in greeting one black visitor at morning worship, and realize that 11 o'clock Sunday morning is still probably the most segregated hour of the week, and that, among all the major institutions in our society, the church is probably still the most segregated.

However, the strongest evidence comes from research studies conducted during the last forty years. People's attitudes towards blacks and other minority groups have been assessed in many different ways, by interviews, by written questionnaires, by observing behavior. The research has been conducted by many different researchers, some of them churchgoers, some of them opposed to the church, most of them disinterested scientific researchers. The research has been done among many different groups of persons, in different regions of this country and in Europe, among different age groups, among persons connected with many different denominations. However and wherever the research has been done, the results have been the same:

• When people are divided between those who say they are church members and those who say they are not, it is the church members who show more evidence of prejudice.

• When people are divided between those who say they attend church and those who do not (membership and attendance are not always the same thing), it is the churchgoers who show more evidence of prejudice.

52

• Those who attend church more regularly, as much as two or three times a month, show more evidence of prejudice than those who attend very seldom. (In the next chapter, we shall see that the story is a little different for those who attend very regularly, weekly or more often.)

• When people are asked how well they believe traditional tests of orthodoxy, such as the virgin birth of Jesus, it is discovered that the more people adhere to such doctrines, the more prejudiced they are.

The Authoritarian Personality illustrates the findings of many such studies. The research team studied persons from many walks of life: workers, students, professional people, prisoners. They asked these people how much they agreed or disagreed with statements such as these:

Negroes have their rights, but it is best to keep them in their own districts and schools and to prevent too much contact with whites.

It would be a mistake ever to have Negroes for foremen and leaders over whites.

Women, if they work at all, should take the most feminine positions, such as nursing, secretarial work, or child care.

One main difficulty with allowing the entire population to participate fully in government affairs is that such a large percentage is innately deficient and incapable.

> The trouble with letting Jews into a nice neighbor-
> hood is that they gradually give it a typical Jewish
> atmosphere.

Each person was asked to indicate whether he agreed with the statement strongly, moderately, or slightly, or whether he disagreed with it slightly, moderately, or strongly. For statistical analysis, these varying degrees of agreement were scored from 1 to 7, with 7 indicating the strongest agreement with the prejudiced statement. 4 would be the neutral point.

When the average opinion for all of the statements for all of the persons was tabulated, these were the results:

All Catholics	4.21
All Protestants	4.01
Non-church members	2.71

In other words, on the average, Catholic and Protestant church members were slightly on the agreement side of neutral with respect to such statements. And those who were not church members, on the average, expressed something between slight and moderate disagreement with such statements. Lutherans showed the highest degree of average agreement (scoring 4.38) even higher than the next highest group, the Mormons (4.23) who include some racial prejudice in their official doctrines.

When people were separated, according to how frequently they said they attended church, the results were as follows:

Regular	3.79
Often	4.14
Seldom	3.94
Never	2.87

Similar results were found when persons were divided between those who reported that their parents were religious and those who reported that their parents were not. And similar results were found when people were divided between those who said that religion and the church were important and those who said they were not. Those who said that religion and the church were both important or "mildly important" showed significantly more prejudice than those who were less enthusiastic about the church.

In this study, the relationship between prejudice and *belief* was discovered, not from questionnaire data, but from interviews with persons. Here is a prime example the authors cite to illustrate how doctrinal convictions are part of the life of one who is also prejudiced. They say that this woman scored high on the prejudice items:

> The subject seems to have accepted a set of rather dogmatic moral codes which makes her regard people, especially "youngsters who call themselves atheists" as falling outside the circle in which she wants to move. She made a point of admitting (confidentially) that one of the main reasons she was looking forward to moving away from Westwood was that she could thereby get her youngest daughter away from the influence of the neigh-

55

bor's boy, who is an atheist because his father tells him "religion is a lot of hooey." She is also distressed, because her eldest daughter "just won't go to church."

From the above it is evident that she is quite in agreement with organized religion and tends to be a conformist in religious matters. Christian ethics and its moral codes are regarded as absolutes; and deviations are to be frowned upon or punished.

Who Are These Churchgoers?

As I grew up in the church, I learned to think of church people as "good" people, and I still do think of them that way. Church people are those whom I learned to regard as pillars of the community, as models for how to live. How could I reconcile this admiration and high regard for churchgoers with such overwhelming evidence of their prejudice? Of course, I could *not* harmonize these two attitudes. At first, I tried to resolve the problem by challenging this unflattering evidence to make it fit my admiring picture of church people. But, much as I examined these research studies for flaws, I could not successfully challenge their results.

Then, it occurred to me that maybe I had the wrong conception of church people. Perhaps church is not for the strong, but for the weak. Perhaps church is not for the saints, but for the sinners. There is, of course, ample biblical precedent for such an understanding. God chose Israel as his people, not because they were established, but because they were wanderers and exiles, not because they were so faithful, but because they were so repeatedly faithless. Jesus spent more time with outcasts than with the established of his society and directed his healing ministry not to the healthy but to the sick. And the best church practice and theological thought see the people of God as the joining together of humble sinners more than the banding together of staunch saints. But still the feeling persists that the body of Christ, the people of God — the church — is and must be the company of the stalwart and strong and respected. Anything less would be unworthy of the Father and our fathers in the faith.

My wife once bought a plaque picturing a household in disarray, which says, "God bless our home. It needs it." That second line seems humorous — maybe even a bit naughty or blasphemous. The second line seems to undo the first line. We have become accustomed to thinking of God's blessing as going along with stable, orderly, well-kept homes and lives. It seems strange to invoke God's blessing because we *need* it.

Our services of worship, too, must be decorous and respectful. All must be hushed when the minister pronounces the invocation at a dinner meeting or business meeting. The spectacle of having a minister pronouncing an invocation at such a disorderly affair as, for example, a political convention, strikes us as incongruous and perhaps worse. God knows, and we know, that a political convention is one of the institutions in our society that most *needs* his blessing. But that isn't what we think of when we see a clergyman mounting the podium at such an occasion. The representative of God seems out of place in a disorderly and noisy arena, precisely the place where he is needed.

Just as we find it incongruous to invoke the presence of God on a disorderly event, we find it equally disconcerting for disorder to enter into the community of the people of God. Selfishness, dispute, antagonism, even honest expression of feelings — such things are often taboo inside the church. An angry voice in a church business meeting seems blasphemous, and the suggestion of prejudice among church members seems especially offensive.

If people show evidence of racial prejudice in the church, it is natural to scold them by saying, "Especially not *here*, especially not *you*." We expect the household of God to be especially in good order and to be the last place we would want to display the prayer, "God bless our home. It needs it."

Our religious style is often like that of Martha who was intent on serving, presumably to make herself and her home suitable for Jesus' presence. We too seldom find ourselves like Mary, simply sitting at Jesus' feet because that is the "one thing needful." It is far easier and more common for us to live with the natural religious notion that we must lift ourselves *up* to God's presence, rather than to live by the Christian affirmation that God comes *down* to us. We still act and feel mostly as though the church is for saints, not for sinners. The church is for the respectable and the healthy and the deserving — that is how we *feel,* even though we really *know* better. We are made uncomfortable, despite ourselves, by any who come to our church because they really need it, or by any suggestion that even we may be in church because we *need* it.

We do know better. The Bible teaches that its message is for the outcasts, the rebels, the faithless, the exiles, those in despair, in prison, hungry, in sin, and in every other way needy. The Jewish people call on the Lord out of their despair in exile and in rebellion — and he answers. From manger to cross, Jesus is the one who is despised and rejected by men, ministering to those who feel despised and rejected. "God bless our home. It needs it," is a proper statement of biblical faith. The fact that it seems humorous and perhaps even blasphemous is a measure of how far most of us have come from that stark faith.

We have analyzed racial prejudice and have found within it a sense of precariousness about life. We have found people feeling at the margins of established society and near the limits of security. We have found people clinging to whatever they can — property, children, anything. And when these start to slip, as they must, we have found people desperately digging in, in ways that foster prejudice. When we have probed prejudice, we have found people feeling in exile or near exile, in despair, insecure and inadequate — and desperately trying to protect themselves from this plight. Should we be surprised, then, if in examining prejudice we also find churchgoing? Is not the church intended to be for those in exile or near exile, in despair, insecure and inadequate? Biblical religion is intended for the people who feel they are on the margins of life, the same people that easily turn to prejudice.

Our success- and achievement- and harmony-oriented American culture does not look kindly on those who admit that they feel threatened, or in despair, or in sin. So, from the perspective of our worldly culture, it seems an insult if we suspect that churchgoers experience more despair and anxiety and sin and sense of marginality and inadequacy than non-churchgoers. But viewed in the perspective of biblical faith, this is precisely what we might expect.

When social scientists have compared churchgoers and non-churchgoers or believers and non-believers, they find results consistent with the biblical expectation. Furthermore, there is a more vigorous religious life in the lower economic levels of our society. Such research is important to us only because it confirms biblical faith's own view: "God bless our home. It needs it."

So it is hardly surprising or offensive, after all, to discover that prejudice is more common among churchgoers than among non-churchgoers. To put the matter another way, *prejudice and churchgoing are both responses to a sense of the precariousness of life.*

There are, of course, two important qualifications to add to such a generalization. The first is that we are dealing only with general tendencies. The correlation between churchgoing and racial prejudice is only a group tendency. Taking large groups of people, there is a tendency to find more prejudice among those who attend church than among those who do not. But this is not to say that any individual churchgoer is more prejudiced than any individual non-churchgoer. There would, of course, be many exceptions.

In the same way, we are generalizing when we say that prejudice arises out of the *need* to defend ourselves in a hostile world or that churchgoing arises directly and solely from that need. In any individual case, prejudice or churchgoing might have quite different roots. Some of us may even go to church occasionally out of a sense of gratitude that our needs have been responded to.

If prejudice and churchgoing are both responses to a sense of need or precariousness, isn't one of them a better response than the other? Is there not some reason to think that the churchgoing may be more satisfactory? If the church can make good on the biblical promise that God does respond to our needs, shouldn't this reduce the needs and, in turn, reduce such desperate responses to our needs — like prejudice? I think that is true. But I also think that the *if* at the beginning of that last sentence is a very large *if*. In any case, the rest of this book will show how the church can respond to people in ways that reduce their racial prejudice.

Does Religion Cause Prejudice?

Churchgoing and prejudice can be best understood as parts of the same iceberg. They are alternative ways in which people respond to similar needs and motives.

Some have suggested that the relationship should be interpreted more directly. They have suggested that if we find more prejudice among churchgoers than non-churchgoers, then there is something about churchgoing that produces the prejudice.

This can be a misleading kind of reasoning. When we see two things together, we tend to jump to the conclusion that one is causing the other. And when we see one before the other, we suppose that the first is causing the second. I was recently riding along a road and noticed a puddle ahead. As I rode through the puddle I felt a deep bump as the wheels dropped into a hole. My first reaction was "That water can certainly eat a big hole in the road!" First I saw the water, then I felt the bump, so my immediate response was to suppose that the one caused the other. Further reflection suggested that maybe it was the other way around, that the hole in the road caused the puddle. Still more reflection suggested to me that it was not so much a matter of one causing the other as of both sharing a common cause. The recent onset of spring, with its alternate thawing and freezing, had done its usual damage to road surfaces, leaving some deep potholes, and it had also produced the runoff of melting snows that yielded the water to fill the pothole.

As a rule, it appears easiest and most natural to suppose that one thing causes another if we see them together. But it also seems a general rule that further reflection is likely to lead us to an understanding of common sources rather than a simple direct influence.

Some writers about religion and prejudice have suggested a simple cause-and-effect relationship. One which attracted much attention is *Christian Beliefs and Anti-Semitism* by Glock and Stark. It proposed the theory that there is something about conventional Christian doctrines that inexorably leads the holder to embrace anti-Semitic prejudices. These writers even go so far as to suggest that an effective way of attacking anti-Semitism is to attack the holding of orthodox Christian beliefs such as those related to the virgin birth. Such thinking has been echoed by another writer Milton Rokeach in the H. Paul Douglass Lectures for 1969.

Some proposals that I regard as more responsible and plausible have been made by Gordon Allport in an article, "The Religious Context of Prejudice." He pointed out that religion introduces elements of exclusiveness. Doctrines of revelation and doctrines of election, for example, lead us to draw boundaries between ourselves and others. And there may be a real sense in which a commitment to faith sometimes needs to be genuinely protected against external threats. There may sometimes be a real need for stockades to protect religion.

On the other hand, maybe this protective emphasis represents only one aspect or one type of religion. Maybe there are other emphases within religion that discourage protectiveness and exclusiveness. With this idea in mind, let us turn to the next chapter and a consideration of two types of religion.

4

Prodigal Faith
and Contractual Faith

Luke records a story we have learned to call the parable of the prodigal son. But it might just as well be called the parable of the prodigal father. Prodigal means extravagant, profuse, lavish, even wasteful and excessive. The son was once prodigal in his spending and in his sinning. But he was also prodigal — excessive, unlimited, unreasonable — in his repentance. And the father was at least as prodigal in his welcome and forgiveness — wasteful beyond any limits of reasonableness or prudence — as his older son was quick to point out. This extravagant prodigality of the father, together with the prodigality of the son's repentance, seems to be the main point of Jesus' parable.

The story contrasts the prodigality of the father with the prudence of the elder brother. Their contrasting responses to the return of the younger son present to us two very different ways of thinking about ourselves and our lives, two very different ways of relating to other people, two very different ways of relating to God.

The older brother is by no means a villain in the story. He is a faithful, dutiful, loving son, as the father clearly affirms. But he understands his relationship with his father — and with his brother — in a way that is different from the way that Jesus wants his hearers to understand their relationship with God their Father. "Lo, these many years I have served you, and I never disobeyed your command." And, in his view, such service and such obedience should be rewarded by the father.

His is a reasonable view and a common one. It is a view that we can all recognize and, for the most part, share. Probably most of our relationships with other persons and most of our religious life is conducted according to the elder brother's precepts. Life is conducted by contract, and the words of the elder brother specified the usual terms of that contract: service and obedience. If I serve and obey my parents, I expect them to reward me; and if I don't, I expect them to punish me. If I serve and obey you, I expect repayment in kind. If I serve and obey God, I expect his reward.

Against this contractual outlook, the father displays a totally different way of understanding life. He is impulsive and extravagant in his outpouring of love and forgiveness. "While he was yet at a distance, his father saw him and had compassion, and ran and embraced him and kissed him. . . . The father said to his servants, 'Bring quickly the best robe, and put it on him; and put a ring on his hand, and shoes on his feet; and bring the fatted calf and kill it, and let us eat and make merry.' " Decorum, prudence, propriety, proportion, even justice — all such considerations are thrown aside in the father's wasteful and prodigal greeting to his son.

The younger son presents his *sinfulness* to his father and is answered not with the response that contract would call for, but by a further squandering of the father's substance. The questions of justice and due considerations are taken up and absorbed in the father's transcendent prodigality.

That is also what happens to the elder brother. When he presents his *goodness* to his father and expects the rewards appropriate to the contract, concerns for justice and proportionality are taken up and absorbed, overwhelmed and transformed, by the father's prodigality. It is not hard to picture the story ending with the father embracing his peevish and pouting elder son with a great bear hug and finally coaxing from him a relaxed face with this prodigal assurance, "Son, you are always with me, and all that is mine is yours."

These two men, elder brother and father, represent two quite different styles of life and of faith, two understandings of how God relates to man and of how man is to relate to God and to his fellowman. We can call these two styles *contractual* and *prodigal*.

This distinction has persistently pervaded Jewish and Christian thought, from earliest times to latest. It is represented powerfully, for example, in the early pages of the Old Testament by the two roles that Moses plays. Moses was lawgiver, the one who brought down the specifications of the contract from the top of Mount Sinai. But even before that, Moses was also liberator. He led his people through the moments of extravagant intervention by God, in plague and in sweeping the Red Sea dry, until they were freed from their enslaving contract in Egypt.

Sometimes the distinction is drawn between the religious emphasis of the Old Testament and the emphasis of the New. The Old Testament emphasizes the covenant between God and man ("I will be your God, and you will be my people") and the detailed prescriptions by which the people were to live up to their part of the bargain; the New Testament emphasizes the absorption of these laws into the new and radical dispensation of grace. (Jesus confuting the Pharisees, picking grain and healing on the Sabbath, saying, "You have heard that it was said . . . but I say to you"; Paul saying "For God has done what the law, weakened by the flesh, could not do.")

The difference is sometimes viewed as the traditional difference between the Protestant emphasis on justification only by faith and the sense of mediated grace which has been strong in the Catholic tradition. In the former style, man is urged to open himself with abandon and without reserve to receive the unreserved and undeserved grace of God, just as the prodigal son opened himself to the prodigal father. In the latter style, man is required to meet the terms of the mediation, to meet the mediator half-way, so to speak, attending the Mass, doing the penance, believing and behaving rightly.

Though there are these traditional differences between Christians and Jews or between Protestants and Catholics on this question, there is also much emphasis within Judaism and within Catholicism on the prodigal style. And, correspondingly, there is within Protestantism a large "good works" component, a conviction that one can, after all, earn salvation by hard work, clean living, and regular church attendance. There is in all religious traditions a strong emphasis on the contractual mode, perhaps because it is easier and more natural. It is easy to expect, with the older brother, that good service and obedience — whether it is burning incense and saying prayers, or doing good deeds and not attending movies on Sunday, or believing the orthodox creeds and scrupulously obeying the Ten Commandments — will have an ultimate payoff.

The difference, in a sense, is the difference between an emphasis on our *doing* and on our *being*. What does God most highly regard and what ought we to regard most highly in ourselves and in others? The contractual mode seems to say that it is what we *do* that most counts. Thus the older brother was so very much aware of how different his doings were from his brother's doings. But the prodigal mode seems to emphasize that important as doing may be, what we *are* is still more important, and that it is in terms of what we are, despite our doings, that we must finally relate to each other and to God. To the prodigal father, both boys were his sons, and *this* is what governed their relationship, not the bad deeds of the one, or the good deeds of the other.

The peril in what is here called the contractual style is not in entering into contracts with men or with God, but in *reliance* on them. The trouble with the older brother is not that he served and obeyed, but that he let these dominate his relationship with his father and his brother. He assumed that serving and obeying, themselves, would earn him the outpouring of his father's substance. We treat these elements of our life and of our religious faith with more reliance than they can stand or repay. They are only elements, but we idolize them and absolutize them. We cling to our good deeds and our good behavior, our service and our obedience, our good works and our lawfulness, as though they could save us.

This, at any rate, is the understanding that people like Paul and Luther have taught us about the prodigal life of grace and faith. They have made clear that elements of works and law have their legitimate, but subordinate, place and become deterrents only as they are relied upon to deliver rewards that are beyond them, as though God could be bound by a contract.

This distinction between prodigal and contractual lifestyles has been discerned by many observers of human experience. Charles Reich in *The Greening of America* distinguishes between Consciousness II and Consciousness III, which corresponds to the distinction between contractual and prodigal styles. Perhaps a more useful analysis is provided by Philip Slater's *In Pursuit of Loneliness*. He suggests that what we have here called the contractual style of life, derives from situations of scarcity, just as the openness we have described as prodigality derives from situations of plenty. It is scarcity that breeds restriction of life, competition, reliance on rules, and obedience to them.

The elder brother who felt deprived of his father's good substance may have been pursuing his dutiful service and scrupulous obedience — his good works and his law — mostly because he felt this deprivation. The younger son had already once experienced the father's prodigality — when he received half his substance — and out of this fullness he felt free not only to follow paths of sin, but also to follow paths of repentance and grace.

Sociologists describe two different kinds of religious organizations, what they call the *church* and the *sect*. The *church* is what most of us know best, the established formal organization, part of a national denomination, with professional well-trained clergy, elaborate national and regional and parish organizations, worship services meeting regularly and properly and decorously. This is truly the *body* of Christ, frequently a very massive and laden body. The *sect* represents more the *spirit* of Christ. Formality is less important than immediate spontaneous expression. Worship is more frequent, more prolonged, much less planned. Worship is not left to the leadership of a few professionals, but is participated in freely by all, not decorously, but with all of their energies. This distinction between church and sect points, in religious organizations and institutions, to some of the same differences we have noted in personal styles of life and faith.

Another useful comparison is with a distinction commonly used by psychologists, the difference between *ego* and *super-ego*. Psychologists use ego to refer to that part of the personality which is most truly and distinctively the self, the person's *identity*. Yet the ego is also that part of the person which is in most complete and harmonious relationship with his environment, with those with whom he lives. In a way analogous to the theologians' understanding of grace and how it works, there is something about an open, even prodigal relationship between the self and the other that most contributes to the development of the self. The younger son riskily opened himself to the world and to his father, and after some serious missteps found his way to the full welcome embrace of his father.

The *super-ego* refers to a set of navigational charts and radar instruments by which a person maneuvers through his environment. Instead of dealing directly and openly — and with risk — with other people and circumstances, he develops a set of rules and procedures by which he governs himself. These rules and procedures are "mediators" and do succeed in helping him to keep on favorable terms with others. But these built-in rules and procedures are also a barrier between himself and full relationship with others, and even a barrier impeding his own self-development. The focus seems to stay on these mediating rules and deflects concern and attention from the person and those he is relating to. One keeps looking at the radar and the navigational charts, so to speak, and misses seeing the waterway itself. For, to change the image, the super-ego may become like a medieval suit of armor. It serves to protect the person rather well, but it also makes it more difficult to move about freely or to greet others.

Researchers have illustrated these two different styles of life and of faith in different ways. How these different perspectives show up in religion has perhaps best been illustrated by *A Study of Generations*. These researchers used a questionnaire of over 700 items to ask nearly 5,000 Lutherans, selected as a representative national sample, almost every imaginable question about their outlook on life and their religion. All of these answers to all of these questions might have arranged themselves in many different patterns. As it turned out, they arranged themselves principally in the pattern suggested by the distinction between the more prodigal, open stance and the more calculating, controlled, contractual stance — between gospel and law as an understanding of God's approach toward them, between faith and good works as an understanding of man's response to God. Chapters 5 and 6 of their report, "The Heart of Lutheran Piety" and "Law-Oriented Lutherans," delineate these two clearly discernible patterns in life and faith.

One pattern emphasized an open and direct and faithful relationship to the transcendent. The other emphasized the importance of a contractual approach, constricting God and one's response to him to those terms and agencies and mediators that can be made precise and measured and controlled. This is the pattern or factor which wants God predictable and under control, subject to contract. Here are some of the phrases with which the researchers characterized this outlook: need for unchanging structure, need for religious absolutism, self-oriented utilitarianism, the exclusive truth claim of Christianity exaggerated, salvation by works, desire for a dependable world.

One more research report can be mentioned here, just because it used different methods with different groups of people, and yet found substantially the same two patterns. V. B. Cline and J. M. Richards Jr. called one pattern the "compassionate samaritan" factor but it seems related to what we are calling the "prodigal" style. Persons strong on this pattern were mostly concerned with interpersonal relations, with "genuine love, compassion, sympathy for others," with living up to the teachings of their religion, and with humility and openness. The other pattern they discovered shows a preoccupation with external forms of religion and with using these religious practices to bolster the security of one's own life. The first pattern discovered by Cline and Richards shows how a person lets religion open himself to others. The other pattern shows how a person uses religion to protect himself.

Prejudice and Contractual Religion

What does all this have to do with prejudice? *Prejudice is associated with contractual religion, not with prodigal religion.* When I said in the last chapter that religious persons were more likely to be prejudiced than others, what I should have said was that persons adhering to a *contractual* religious outlook were more likely to be prejudiced than others. To test this statement, divide the churchgoers you know into those whose outlook on religion and life seems mostly contractual, and those whose outlook on religion and life seems more open and prodigal. (Perhaps you could also devise a way to divide a group of non-churchgoers between those who are mostly contractual and mostly prodigal in their style of life.) Now you will find that prejudice, and all the things that we have said are likely to go with prejudice, are far more likely to be found among the contractual group, rather than the other.

Or perhaps it is misleading to talk about separating persons into the two groups. Perhaps we should talk about different tendencies within each one of us. Each of us has some inclinations to be contractual in outlook and other inclinations to be prodigal and open.

The prejudice within each of us is likely to be related to the contractual orientation within each of us.

When we peel down the prejudice we find in ourselves, one of the things we find is this contractual orientation, an inclination to make deals with God and with others, an inclination to suppose that our salvation and well-being can be guaranteed by dutiful compliance with one or another obligation, performance of one or another law, demonstration of one or another set of good works. (Perhaps it is necessary to keep reminding ourselves that what is most important about the contractual orientation is not that we undertake to obey laws or to perform good works, but rather that we tend to escalate laws and good works to a more ultimate significance than they deserve, to rely on them for a salvation and assurance that they cannot deliver. We become addicted to our rules and to our deals. It is this *addiction* that we most need to notice in connection with the contractual orientation.)

It may seem especially understandable that prejudice is present where contractual religion is present when we recognize that prejudice, after all, has a close family resemblance to contractual religion. An act of prejudice resembles an act of contractual religion in many respects. In a moment of contractual religion, we are taking the unfathomable mysteries of God and his relations with us and collapsing them into a deed (e.g., church-going) or an object (e.g., rosary) or a rule (e.g., "don't drink") which *is* fathomable and manageable, but which is now too constricted to be treated as God. But we still treat this constricted form with the awe and trust that is appropriate only for the God that transcends all such forms. In a moment of prejudice, we are collapsing the rich unfathomable mysteries of other persons into sterotypes or pictures or labels that can be managed, to our benefit, but which bear little resemblance to the real persons. The prejudiced mind and the contractual mind — like the elder brother — constrict their experience and their world to narrow and familiar boundaries that they can patrol and control.

Among the officials of the Augustana Church (A Time for Burning) and among the trustees of the Bethany Church, we can see some of this contractual approach. There is a preoccupation with "our church" and its stability, in which the church seems to become not so much an instrument of God but a stand-in for God. Some have the attitude that the present organization and tranquility of persons in the church must not be disrupted, that existing budgets and procedures are sacrosanct. We get the impression that people feel this way about their church, whatever question may come up. There is in this attitude largely the same constriction, the same huddling behind a stockade that is in prejudice and racial exclusion.

If there is a family resemblance between prejudice and contractual religion, there also appears to be a common ancestry. If the *what* appears to be similar, so does the *why*. We seem to need prejudice and contractual religion for the same reason. We use them for the same purpose. Both prejudice and various forms of contractual religion hold out the promise or protection and assurance of worth and of an established place in the universe. Prejudice helps us to place ourselves and to place ourselves high, by placing others down. Contractual religion helps us to place ourselves with confidence as meriting high regard in the eyes of God and in the eyes of others. Both result from an uneasiness and insecurity about ourselves and our fate which is apparently not experienced so keenly by those with a more "prodigal" religion. Both reflect the fretfulness of the elder brother until he experiences and believes the embracing assurance of his father, "Son, you are always with me, and all that is mine is yours."

The Evidence of Research Studies

Several research studies illustrate that prejudice is associated with contractual religion and not with prodigal religion. Perhaps most dramatic is that evidence provided by *A Study of Generations.* Chapter 1 described some of the measures of prejudice used in this research. Earlier in this chapter, we referred to this study's demonstration of two styles of religion. It remains now to point out how clearly and decisively this research found that prejudice was related only to the one style of religion, called here contractual, and called by the researchers "law orientation." All measures indicating prejudice were intimately embedded in the many measures of "law orientation," but had no part of the dimension regarded as "the heart of Lutheran piety."

Another thorough research study, T. C. Campbell and Yoshio Fukuyama's *The Fragmented Layman,* was completed with members of United Church of Christ, a group quite different from the Lutherans in heritage and outlook. This research was based on questionnaires completed by more than 8,000 members. It measured racial attitudes in ways similar to that of *A Study of Generations.* Researchers asked how closely persons would accept Negroes, whether as church members, as guests in the home, as neighbors, as personal friends. They also asked about opinions towards the civil rights of blacks. Evidence of prejudice on such measures correlated with only *some* measures of religion, the measures that seem to me to suggest the contractual style. For example, prejudice was correlated with adherence to such precise statements of doctrine as "Hell is just punishment for sinners," or "Jesus was born of a virgin." The authors call these "very particularized statements of the Christian faith." But *favorable* attitudes towards blacks were correlated with *other* indications of religious involvement. Most notable was a concern for the devotional life. Persons who thought that prayer and devotional life were important were more likely to hold favorable and tolerant attitudes towards blacks.

Finally, we can look back at the data from the study of *The Authoritarian Personality* on page 55. The second set of numbers there reports that those who attend church tend to be more prejudiced than those who do not. But now look more carefully at the very top line, "Regular" churchgoers scored 3.79, less than "often" or "seldom" attenders. The prejudice score is somewhat *less* for those who attend *most* often. This difference is important because it has been found in many research studies. It is found for example in the study of members of the United Church of Christ by Campbell and Fukuyama. And it has been found in studies of members of many different churches. Those who attend church on a weekly basis — faithfully, we are tempted to say — consistently show less evidence of prejudice than those who attend, but less regularly.

What does this mean? Why do people attend church every week without fail? One *could* suppose that this is an especially strong form of contractual religion, that people are offering this obedient duty and service to God, in hopes of sure reward. Or one could surmise that such thoroughly "faithful" attendance, as we say, reflects a different style of religion. Perhaps duty and obedience do not get people to church every week, but almost every week. Perhaps such regular weekly attendance reflects a faith more thoroughly and intimately integrated into one's life. Perhaps it reflects the religious posture of the prodigal son, after his reassuring forgiveness and welcome by his prodigal father. Feeling this assurance might make one no longer need the pseudo-assurance provided by his racial prejudices, and might make one no longer need the pseudo-assurance provided by his dutiful performance of contracts with God, but might make one want to express fully and regularly his sense of his membership in God's family.

With this in mind, let us now consider ways in which the church may do something to reduce prejudice.

5

Overcoming Prejudice

Let me remind you of the four incidents described at the beginning of this book:

1. Someone tells you, "Negroes could solve many of their own problems if they would not be so irresponsible and carefree about life."

2. Church members and officials of the Augustana Church object to a plan for an interracial exchange of home visits.

3. A regular churchgoer says about a black woman visitor one Sunday morning, "I wanted to say hello to her, but didn't quite know how to do it. So I found myself going out the other door."

4. Bethany Church trustees oppose a Christian Education committee plan to give a $100 scholarship to an inner-city boy for a summer conference.

Suppose you are present on these occasions and recognize elements of racial prejudice in them. The speakers are constricting their lives and being less than the full and loving persons they are created to be. They are constricting their relations with others and making these relations less abundant and loving than they are intended to be. They are constricting and hurting others' lives. Suppose, therefore, you feel called to say something or to do something that will reduce the prejudice. What will you do?

I think that what you would *do* will depend largely on how you *see* the situation. My hope is that the previous four chapters in this book may make a difference in how you do *see* these episodes.

Overwhelming the Prejudice

Probably your first reaction, and mine, is to focus in on the wrongs, the factual wrongs and the moral wrongs, and to correct them. We can argue against the misstatements of facts and the faulty reasoning. We can protest the narrow sentiments and urge people to be less selfish and bigoted. If someone says that Negroes are irresponsible, we can point to the evidence against this generalization. If someone says that black people could solve many of their own problems, we can point out how many of their problems are the fault of institutions that are controlled by whites. If someone says that December is too busy, we point out that there is always time for something important. If a trustee says that the plan is too controversial and will split the church, we point out that it is really a very small step and argue that most church members will support it; and even if they don't, the church still must do what is right or it is not the church and ought not to survive. If someone argues that racial integration reduces property values, we cite the evidence that proves this is not so. If someone says she feels uncomfortable greeting a black visitor, we reply, "But don't you think you should, anyhow. Think how *she* feels." If someone argues that black girls at camp seem to prefer to stay by themselves, we can reply that this is because they have been made to feel so separated and that this proves all the more the need for overcoming the separation. If someone objects to using Christian Education committee money for "outsiders," we dig up the precedent of the time the neighboring suburban church was invited to send children to our summer Bible school, without charge for them.

So it goes. Each argument that seems to convey some racial prejudice can be countered with other arguments, with appeals to facts, with appeals to moral principles. Though many of our arguments will provoke counter arguments, some of our arguments will win out, and our opponent will concede our point: December *is* acceptable, one *should* greet a visitor, etc. But even after we win the argument, somehow the opposition and the prejudice seem to persist. The abandoned arguments give way to new ones. We are chipping away at the top of the iceberg, and even when we get the visible ice chopped away, suddenly more ice rises up to take its place. This is exactly what the minister was doing in *A Time for Burning,* and this is exactly what he experienced. We do not really affect the prejudice that is below the surface when we attack the arguments that make it visible.

So we can escalate our attack and try to chop away at the prejudice below the surface. We can attack more directly the prejudice which is producing the arguments in the opposition. We can scold people for their prejudice — and we are right in this judgment. We can cajole and rally votes to get our program through, and we can win the vote and introduce the program. But still there is more iceberg. We can blast away all expression of prejudice in a particular meeting, but the prejudice persists in the person. We can affect his vote, but only his vote is affected; he is not. Prejudice remains deeply motivated and strongly entrenched.

In our frustration, we are driven to still higher escalation, attacking persons more and more strongly, until eventually we disrupt relationships and destroy or abandon the church.

Sometimes I try to imagine how God must have felt just before the time of the New Testament. The Old Testament could be taken as a record of just this kind of escalating but futile confrontation — on a somewhat more momentous scale, indeed, than a trustees' meeting in the Bethany or Augustana church. From the first misdeed in the Garden of Eden on through mounting faithlessness and sin by God's people, these erring people are held up to law and judgment — by new regulations and sanctions, by exile and by flood, by shrill prophetic voices, by prototypes of all the arguments we might muster in a trustees' meeting — all to little avail and to enhanced frustration.

It was at that point, I am reminded in my fantasy, that God tried a new method: instead of trying to scold and punish and threaten people out of their erring ways, he decided to come down and enter into their erring ways. The move from the top of Sinai to a manger in Bethlehem and a cross on Golgotha is a drastic change of strategy in the history of God's redemptive purposes. The change perhaps suggests a change of strategy in our own approach to meeting prejudice.

Overwhelming the Person

Our attempts to undo prejudice by attacking it and the people who hold it are not only futile. More often than not, our attacks on prejudice actually increase the prejudice by increasing peoples' *need* for the prejudice.

Consider Paul's understanding of the law: "law came in, to increase the trespass," Romans 5:20. The law was right and good; so is our attack on prejudice right and good, holding it up against the plumbline of God's intentions. But the law enhances the very sin it would judge. *The more we attack directly another's prejudice and try to revise his attitudes, the more we seem to be enhancing exactly those feelings of precariousness and desperation which breed prejudice.*

I once watched children playing with a young kitten and some string. The kitten ignored the string, much to the consternation of the children. They were determined to exercise a ministry to the kitten to help it realize its kittenhood. They responded directly to the defect and set out to remedy it directly, just as we respond to the defects in each other and, with the best of intentions, endeavor to remedy the defects directly. They took the kitten's paw and made it bat at the string. As long as they controlled the kitten's paw in their own hands, the paw was batting at the string, and all seemed well — just as sometimes we can, with our arguments or other power, control what people say and how they vote in a meeting, so that all seems well. But the kitten was not really changed, just as people are not really changed by such direct manipulation. Indeed, the kitten was not only not learning to play with the string; it was, in fact, learning to exert all its energies to pull away from the string. In struggling to protect itself from the direct "ministry" of the children, the kitten was also pulling away from the intended object of that "ministry." So it frequently is with our efforts to remedy prejudice by overwhelming it. We end up by overwhelming the person and increasing the need for the prejudice.

Transmitting the Need for Prejudice

Let us look again at the distinction between contractual and prodigal religion and then notice this perplexing and frustrating irony: our own efforts to undo another's prejudice almost always become law with its demands and threats, not gospel with its freedom and assurance. We do to him what his prejudice does to others. We transmit fear, threat, and disdain for personal worth.

As we have seen, the prejudiced person is constricting others' lives (and his own) as a way of building a security and sense of well-being in his own life. This prejudice is one of his responses to his sense of the precariousness of those values and gods by which he lives. He lives in a fearful, contractual world which imposes impossible, non-win contracts on him: *do this* and *be that* if you want to be well regarded. Prejudice becomes one of the ways he can negotiate new contracts that he can win ("I will huddle with people designated as 'good' and compare myself with those who are inferior"); and in so doing, he imposes new non-win impossible contracts on others (for example, "You must be white in skin and manner, if you want my regard"). The prejudice, then, transmits to others his own fearful sense of living under the demand of contracts that he cannot meet.

This also seems to be what we often do when we set out to "minister" to other people by undoing their prejudices. Changing another's attitudes, or getting him to support my program so easily becomes a way for me to score points for myself. Undoing his prejudice becomes a "good work" of my own, a way of making me feel that I am meeting the demands of a contract imposed on me. I am most likely to need this "good work" when I most feel inadequate in terms of the expectations and "laws" by which I am living my life.

One of the most dramatic scenes in *A Time for Burning* is the confrontation between the black barber and the white minister. The barber flays the minister with a recital of the sins of the white man, and especially the white church, and especially the white ministers. His indictments are on target and are delivered with a cool power. I don't know how this prophetic tongue-lashing made the minister feel, but I know how it made me feel. It made me feel guilty. It made me feel like a failure. If I had been that minister, I would have left that barber shop feeling a desperate need to achieve visible results in my church, results that could make up for the feelings of failure. In this sense, I would be "needing" these results, and any opposition to my plans would be dealt with in terms of my frustration.

Frequently my concern to change another's prejudice is, in actuality, asking him to minister to me, rather than to be serving as a minister to him. My needs, growing out of my own sense of failure, lead me to impose new demands, to represent the world of contract and law, on another. He is just as certain to experience frustration and failure, as judged by these new demands, as I was; and this failure and frustration will lead him to need to *increase* his prejudice, as a way of coping with this new failure.

The prejudiced person is addicted to his particular narrow view of life because it does something for him. He needs it. When I set out to reform the prejudice, my reform ambitions also can easily become a narrowed view of life; I can easily become addicted to them, because they do something for me. I need the reform. The paradox and the tragedy is that I may need the reform so desperately that I impose it on the other so ruthlessly that it makes him need the comfort of his prejudice all the more.

Undermining the Prejudice

Christian faith says to the prejudiced person: your prejudice is wrong, and we need to say this to each other (as I have said, for example, in the opening paragraphs of Chapters 1 and 3). But Christian faith has much more to say to the prejudiced person. And there is much more that we need to say and do for each other, if we are to represent the Christian faith for each other. There is much more we can do for the iceberg of prejudice than to try to chop away at the blocks of ice that show. If we can melt the iceberg from the bottom, we dispose of it much more decisively. Although Christian faith can and ought to say that the expression of the prejudice is wrong, Christian faith can also announce powerfully and uniquely that the *need* for the prejudice does not exist.

Christian faith says to the prejudiced person: "You may feel that your life, your well-being, your worth are guaranteed by the stockades (including prejudice) you have built and by those treasures you are protecting with your stockade — social status, signs of personal success, accomplished children, or whatever other merits. But your worth is not guaranteed by these things; they are too feeble. More importantly, your personal worth does not need such fragile guarantees. It is already guaranteed by One whose guarantee is unchallengeable and unchallenging."

Christian faith also says to the prejudiced person: "You may feel that your well-being and personal worth are reduced by the threats and failures that you experience and that you need to make up for these failures by your own maneuvers — such as the maneuvers of prejudice and discrimination. But you cannot 'make good' in this way, and, more importantly, you do not need to. The threats and failures you experience do not challenge your well-being and personal worth in any significant sense. This is guaranteed by One whose assurance is unchallengeable and unchallenging."

This is what the Christian faith says to the prejudiced person. It is up to those of us who would be Christians to make this affirmation alive and credible for one another.

When we set out to *overwhelm* the prejudice, to chop away at the visible part of the iceberg, we are usually responding in terms of what the prejudice means to us, as agents of a contractual religion. We are wondering what we can do about the prejudice that will help us meet the conditions of our own contract. If we want to undermine the prejudice, to melt away the base of the iceberg, we respond in terms of what it means to the person who holds it. As agents of a prodigal religion, wanting to open life to others, we can try to look more deeply inside the prejudice. We can try to decode the expression of prejudice and discover the needs and anxieties it represents, and we can try to respond to these. In the one case, my attention is on the other's deeds and "works," as a way of achieving my own "good works." In the other way, my attention is on *him*, with a desire to share with him the trust and faith I feel.

Sharing my faith, melting the base of the iceberg, I can expect with some confidence that the prejudice will be affected in desirable ways. But this is not the prime purpose of my intervention. I do not *need* his conversion of attitude. We can suppose that the prodigal son found a responsible role in the household after his prodigal welcome home, but getting him back to work on the farm was *not* the purpose of the welcome. He was welcomed, for *himself*, not for any dutiful obedience he would henceforth deliver to his father.

Transforming Losers and Loners

What does prejudice do for a person? The Christian community can do it better, more reliably, and without the cost of the damage and hurt that prejudice inflicts on others.

Does racial prejudice make me feel an importance and worth I would not otherwise feel, by drawing sharp contrasts between myself and others whom I have deemed unworthy? The Christian community, at its best, makes me feel such importance and worth more profoundly and more securely, when it offers me the same ennobling and enabling embrace the prodigal father offered both his sons.

Does prejudice make me feel powerful, when I would otherwise feel powerless and vulnerable? Does prejudice permit me to feel the defensive power of the stockade and the aggressive power of dominating other's lives? The Christian community can make me feel the kind of ever-fresh, ever-surprising power that comes from opening myself to the infinite riches of God's creation and to my many marvelous fellow creatures, and, through the majesty of the creation, to the Creator himself.

Does prejudice make me feel a winner by letting me arrange my world so that I come out on top when I would otherwise feel a loser? The Christian community can help me to rediscover that the categories of winning and losing by which I am feeling judged are the transient categories of the culture in which I live. They are not God's terms for life. Western culture's preoccupation for "winning" in its many forms comes to an apex in contemporary American life. But God's answer to this preoccupation comes to an apex on the cross.

Does prejudice make me feel that I really belong to a group of people, when I would otherwise feel keenly my isolation and loneliness? Does prejudice enable me to build a sense of group solidarity, by huddling with my fellows in prejudice, and by making our closeness seem artificially great by contrast with the separation we impose on others? The Christian community can find ways, in small groups and large, to make me feel that I truly belong with and for others.

Does prejudice make me feel that I have a place in the universe after all, when I would otherwise feel a wandering fugitive? Does prejudice stabilize an otherwise turbulent world by marking out clear though artificial boundaries? The Christian community can find ways to assure me that it is precisely wandering fugitives and exiles who have a place in the universe, that those who build towers of Babel and who count up their treasures in their barns are only deceiving themselves.

Does prejudice help me to cope with the terrifying world by making the world much, much smaller and enclosed? Does prejudice help me to cope with a terrifying world by imposing on it a rigid grid? The Christian community can point to evidence that the world is not terrifying, that it is good *in* its richness and openness and prodigal creativity. The Christian community can help me to discover that I don't have to manage the world and that I cannot manage the world, because it is already well-managed.

Does prejudice make me to feel that I can save myself by damning others? The Christian community helps me to discover that I cannot and need not save myself. That has already been done.

How can a Christian minister and a Christian community respond to the prejudiced Bethany trustees or the prejudiced Augustana board, or the fearful woman going out the side door rather than greeting a black visitor? The Christian community can move beyond the wrong in this attitude and behavior and can recognize the desperation that lies behind the attitude and behavior. The community can try to accept this desperation, not enhance it. The community, like the prodigal father, can transform this desperation by embracing it.

In the meeting, the trustee can be answered, "I can understand how upset you are by this proposal," or "I can see that this means a lot to you." Perhaps the trustee responds by talking then about what upsets him — unpeeling the prejudice — perhaps later, perhaps not at all. But the prejudice is being undermined. Such a response as "I can understand how upset you feel" may not be as dramatic or as redemptive as the killing of the fatted calf, but it is a gesture of prodigal embrace, nevertheless, and has a freeing assurance. There will be other meetings, too, in which the anxieties can be discerned and lifted up to redemptive light. There will be resources, too, of scripture and preaching, group life and prayer, work projects and service which can be addressed more accurately to the needs of the trustee, once those needs are discerned in his prejudicial outburst.

Feeling the Urgency

To respond to prejudice in this "prodigal" way seems to many people to be puny and weak and futilely indirect. They would say: the problem is far too serious and devastating not to act massively and directly against it. I would say: the problem is far too serious and devastating not to act as effectively as our deepest insights permit. The problem is too serious and devastating for us to indulge our own needs for being strong. The Christian gospel is too powerful and too true to permit us to be worried anyhow about what is puny and what is strong.

When Mrs. Simpson first said to me "I wanted to say hello to her, but didn't quite know how to do it," my reaction was a muddled mixture of feelings. Her attitude seemed to me wrong, and I felt an obligation to say so; I suddenly felt looking over my shoulder all the preachers and teachers and black friends who urged me to stand up against racial wrongs. And I felt my own commitment to oppose such wrongs. I wanted to take the side of the black lady and scold Mrs. Simpson for slighting her. I thought of getting a dozen black friends to come to church next week — too many for Mrs. Simpson to avoid. That would make her shape up, and be something I could boast to my liberal friends about!

But Mrs. Simpson is a strong woman, not easily "reshaped." And I was both weary and wary from previous encounters. Besides, I wondered, perhaps to justify my timidity, what right had I to "reshape" her? My own greeting to the black visitor had been largely perfunctory and duty-bound. So my first response was a bland cover over all these confused reactions — avoiding all the issues — something like, "Well, she did get away pretty fast herself." I couldn't face any of these confused reactions and weaknesses in myself any better than Mrs. Simpson could.

Then, it occurred to me, in what could perhaps really be called a religious experience, that all my confusion and sense of failure and frustration wasn't so bad. This muddle wasn't so bad that I couldn't confess it openly to myself, to God, and to Mrs. Simpson. Why not level with her? "I think I know how you feel. I find it tough sometimes to open up and talk with people in important ways. Even right now, I suppose, it would be easier not to have to stand here and talk to each other about tough things." She didn't say much then, mostly ducked out.

But from then on, she and I had a special bond, and even a private language. "Out the back door, or talk it out?" she startled me one evening when a committee was politely arguing about something. And we talked it out there and felt a grace and have felt a prodigality in each others' lives at other points.

It would be tempting to find a way to end the incident with a glorious account of "success" in changing Mrs. Simpson's racial attitudes and to report that she opened her life and her home and her church to people she had once excluded. I think she probably has. But somehow, at the same time that such changes become more real, it seems less important to "keep score" of them. Life does not have to be lived by doing and saying the right thing and counting up our successes. Openness, the undoing of prejudice, is not a task, but a gift.

Bibliography

Adorno, T. W.; Frenkel-Brunswik, Else; Levinson, Daniel J.; and Sanford, R. Nevitt. *The Authoritarian Personality.* New York: Harper, 1950.

Allen, Russell O., and Spilka, Bernard. "Committed and Consensual Religion: A Specification of Religion-Prejudice." *Journal for the Scientific Study of Religion* (1967) **6**: 191-206.

Allport, Gordon W. *The Nature of Prejudice.* Cambridge, Mass.: Addison-Wesley, 1954.

——————. "The Religious Context of Prejudice." *Journal for the Scientific Study of Religion* (1966) **5**: 447-458.

Allport, Gordon W., and Kramer, B. M. "Some Roots of Prejudice." *Journal of Psychology* (1946) **22**: 9-39.

Campbell, Thomas C., and Fukuyama, Yoshio. *The Fragmented Layman.* Philadelphia: Pilgrim Press, 1970.

101

Cline, V. B., and Richards, J. M. Jr. "A Factor Analytic Study of Religious Belief and Behavior." *Journal of Personality and Social Psychology* (1965) 1: 569-578.

Dittes, James E. *The Church in the Way*. New York: Scribner's, 1967.

Glock, Charles Y., and Stark, Rodney. *Christian Beliefs and Anti-Semitism*. New York: Harper and Row, 1966.

Hartley, E. L. *Problems in Prejudice*. New York: King's Crown Press, 1946. Octagon Books, 1970.

Reich, Charles. *The Greening of America*. New York: Random House, 1970.

Rokeach, Milton. *The Open and Closed Mind*. New York: Basic Books, 1960.

—————. "The H. Paul Douglass Lectures for 1969." *Review of Religious Research* (1969) 11: 3-39.

Slater, Philip. *The Pursuit of Loneliness*. Boston: Beacon Press, 1970.

Strommen, Merton P.; Brekke, Milo L.; Underwager, Ralph C.; and Johnson, Arthur L. *A Study of Generations*. Minneapolis: Augsburg, 1972.